Better Allies®

PRAISE FOR *BETTER ALLIES*®

"I tore through *Better Allies*, and you will too. Karen Catlin has brought clarity to the challenges underrepresented people face at work. Read this book if you want advice on how to be a better ally, on how to create a more inclusive culture, and on how to increase your competitive advantage around hiring and retaining talent."
—Norm Meyrowitz
former President of Products, Macromedia

"Calling all allies! Here is your one-stop manual for becoming better as an advocate, champion, and ally for marginalized colleagues in the workplace. Catlin's rich experience as an executive in the tech world infuses each of her immensely practical allyship strategies with deep wisdom from the trenches. This amazing book is both an invitation and a roadmap to every person and organization committed to making the workplace fully inclusive."
—Brad Johnson, PhD and **David G. Smith, PhD**
authors of *Athena Rising* and *Good Guys*

"Some people have it harder than you at work. This is just true. Get over it. And, yes, there are many permutations of this dynamic involving class, color, race, sexual orientation and a few thousand other ways people are different from each other. We tend to not notice it, or not do anything about it, at least partly because we're not sure what to do. Fortunately, we now have *Better Allies*. It's incredibly complete and packed with practical advice to help you start to make a difference in your organization."
—Joe Dunn
Executive Coach and Radical Candor Guru

"As a global business strategist with a plural board career, I am passionate regarding how imperative it is in today's world that companies must sharpen their competitive advantage by attracting and retaining top talent. *Better Allies* is a thoughtful and insightful book, offering a tool kit of meaningful, actionable ideas for the reader of how to create a meaningful and engaging workplace." **—Eugenia Ulasewicz**
former President, Burberry America

"Navigating today's business landscape requires everyone to build their ability to support colleagues and coach others. This book will give you valuable insights and practical advice on being a better ally. It's an eye-opening, powerful approach."
—Tom Hale
President, SurveyMonkey

"Karen Catlin has created an accessible, practical everyday guide to becoming a better ally. Whether you are just starting out or you've been an ally for years, everyone can learn something new from this terrific book." **—Elizabeth Ames**
CEO, Women In Product

"*Better Allies* is an important book for outcome-focused executives, however we classify ourselves. As someone who mentors a broad set of up-and-coming product managers and product leaders, I see every day how urgently we need to widen our lenses to spot emerging talent we've often overlooked — even as so many product leadership roles remain unfilled. Karen Catlin provides a range of actionable, motivating, effective tools for growing more diverse teams so that we can deliver more successful products. *Better Allies* can help each of us be better allies." **—Rich Mironov**
startup CEO and author of *The Art of Product Management*

"Ever found yourself wondering 'How can I better support diversity and inclusion in the workplace?' In *Better Allies*, Karen Catlin breaks it down and helps to guide the conversation. This book is just the beginning of a grassroots movement. And it's going to help make a big difference to workplaces everywhere." **—Brad Arkin**
Chief Security and Trust Officer, Cisco

"As businesses continue to focus on local and global expansion, I believe success lies in seeking and embracing differing cultural perspectives. The first step is to have a workforce which is reflective of their target customer. By including and advocating for people of all genders, cultures and lifestyles, and ensuring they are reflected in all levels of the company from the board room to the mail room, businesses will develop a practice of empathy and understanding which will translate into more meaningful connections, thus products and services people believe in. Better Allies paves a road to this success." **—Steve Johnson**
Vice President of Experience Design and Innovation, Netflix

"As men, we have a whole lot of privilege. And we can use that privilege to open doors and bring more diversity into 'the room where it happens.' In *Better Allies*, you'll learn practical steps to do exactly that and create a more inclusive workplace. Be a better man and read this book now." **—Ray Arata**
Co-Founder, Inclusionary Leadership Group

ALSO BY KAREN CATLIN

The Better Allies® Approach to Hiring

Present! A Techie's Guide to Public Speaking
(with Poornima Vijayashanker)

Better Allies®

Everyday Actions to Create Inclusive, Engaging Workplaces

Second Edition

KAREN CATLIN

Better Allies Press

Published by Better Allies Press.
www.betterallies.com

SECOND EDITION, January 2021

Hardcover ISBN: 978-1-7327233-4-4
Softcover ISBN: 978-1-7327233-5-1

Editing: Sally McGraw
Cover design: Melissa Tenpas
Illustrations on back cover, Chapters 12-13: Danielle Coke

Icons in Chapter 1: from the "Noun Project" by Adrien Coquet, Dinosoft Labs, unlimicon, Thomas' designs, ProSymbols, Ben Davis, and corpus delicti. Licensed under Creative Commons CC BY 3.0.

Author's site: www.karencatlin.com

CONTENTS

AUTHOR'S NOTE

Remaining attuned to our own words — especially when we use names and terms to describe people from groups that we ourselves don't belong to — is a crucial and complex part of being an ally. While I was writing this second edition of *Better Allies*, the conversation around the words that are used to describe non-white groups of people was actively evolving. I noticed some authors using BIPOC, which stands for Black, Indigenous, and People of Color. I also saw posts by Black people whom I respect saying that they didn't want this label to be applied to them. They were Black, not BIPOC. The conversations that I read were nuanced and impassioned, but I didn't see much consensus. Which is understandable, since this is a matter that affects multiple, extremely varied populations, and affects them deeply.

So, I decided to refer to specific races where appropriate. For example, I say "A Black person" when talking specifically about a Black person. If I need to refer to a more generalized group of people who aren't white, I use the phrase "BIPOC" although there has been some pushback against this term, too. When I quote research that refers to "people of color," I will use that phrase to mirror the authors' language. You'll also see that I capitalize Black (when talking about race), while making white lowercase. I'm following the AP Style Guide.[1]

My decisions and approach are informed (shout out to both my friend Dr. Suzanne Wertheim and NPR's Code Switch podcast[2]) yet imperfect. By the time this book reaches your hands, the conversation may have taken a turn in a totally new direction. But, as with everything in allyship, I am choosing to do what seems best right now, knowing that I may learn more later and make different, better choices then.

—Karen

INTRODUCTION

A diverse and inclusive workplace has a certain buzz about it. Employees are thriving, and they love their work. Engagement survey scores are through the roof. People from different backgrounds, races, ethnicities, genders, sexual orientations and identities, ages, and abilities are hired and set up for success — and they want their friends to work there too, because their experience is so positive.

Unfortunately, diverse and inclusive workplaces are elusive. They are both difficult to find and hard to create. Leaders struggle to create internal policies that are truly equitable, HR departments scramble to create recruiting and hiring tactics that attract people from underrepresented groups, and employees endeavor to build welcoming and accepting corporate cultures. It all feels complex and cumbersome, to the point that many would rather opt out than risk making a diversity-related faux pas.

Opting out, however, is not an option. Building workplaces that are bursting with employees from underrepresented groups and informed allies who support them is more important than ever. In the wake of the killings of Breonna Taylor and George Floyd, and after so many other Black lives have been lost due to police brutality, people in the United States and around the world have a greater energy and focus on not allowing the status quo to prevail. They want to see an end to systemic racism. Many people are protesting. Many are donating to charitable causes related to Black Lives Matter. Many are using their vote to elect new leaders, hoping for new policies and laws. Some of that energy has begun to spill over into workplaces, where business leaders are making long-overdue commitments to diversity and inclusion. I'm seeing changes to annual goals, org charts, interviewing tactics, benefits policies, supply chains, charitable giving, and more. It's encouraging to see more organizations focusing on equity and diversity in meaningful ways.

Yet there are still miles to go. The evidence of bias and oppression is both codified and anecdotal. Research has revealed the extent of the barriers faced by Black and Brown people, women, LGBTQ people, people with disabilities, and members of other underrepresented groups in the workplace — from being consistently underhired, overlooked, and excluded from professional opportunities to being subjected to harassment and abuse on the job. What's more, people in positions of privilege are often unaware of the issues facing underrepresented groups working in their industry.

My own observations about these worrying trends come from 25 years of working in the tech industry. I remember having a wake-up call when I was a vice president of engineering at Adobe. While I was keenly aware that women had little chance of breaking into senior leadership roles, many of my male colleagues were oblivious. They firmly believed Adobe was a meritocracy. They told me it was the kind of company where all genders had an equal chance of getting ahead and clung to this belief even though our demographics proved otherwise. Men dominated the senior leadership roles across the organization, and although according to my calculations at the time, women made up a third of the company's directors and senior directors, that number dropped to just 18 percent at the vice president level.

I began to see discrimination bubbling up in overt and covert ways. I remember talking with a man on my staff who needed to fill a senior role on his team. When I asked if he planned to promote his top employee into the role, he replied that she had young children at home and he felt sure that she wouldn't want all the travel that would come with the promotion. I countered, saying that this was her decision to make, not his. (He decided to make her the offer, which she accepted. She went on to totally rock the role.)

Then there was the 2014 Grace Hopper Celebration of Women in Computing, a troubling moment for gender diversity in tech. At the event, Satya Nadella, the newly appointed CEO of Microsoft, proclaimed that women shouldn't ask for raises. Instead, he suggested that they should have faith and wait for the system to give them the pay rates they deserved.[3] This advice was perplexing to women in the audience who worked in an industry where they earned between 4 percent and 45 percent less than men in the same roles.[4] Despite being constantly overlooked and underpaid, the advice they were being given was to sit on their hands? They charged back on social media, and Nadella soon apologized.

But that wasn't all. The conference also featured a male allies panel. Men from Facebook, Google, Intuit, and GoDaddy shared what they had done to improve gender diversity within their prominent companies. Unfortunately, the panel missed its mark. The speakers were clueless about the challenges women faced, reiterating tired platitudes about how hard work pays off and how confidence is a huge asset to working women.[5] It was a disaster, and one that enraged people of all genders.

As the years rolled by, appalling statistics about the hiring and promotion of BIPOC[i] in my industry surfaced. A 2017 report by the Ascend Foundation included data from hundreds of Silicon Valley companies, including Apple, Cisco, Facebook, Google, HP, Intel, Twitter, and Yelp, and showed that race is an increasingly more significant impediment than gender to climbing the management ladder.[6] That same year, Recode reported that Black and Latinx[ii] employees held only 4 percent to 10 percent of leadership roles at seven major tech companies.[7] This all came to light in the wake of tech companies prioritizing growth over everything else, even when it enabled discrimination. For example, Nextdoor users are notorious for posting racist "crime and safety" alerts targeting their neighbors of color, and Airbnb found that "guests with 'distinctively African American names' are 16% less likely to be accepted than identical guests with white-sounding names."[8] It seemed that the tech industry was unaware of its ingrained racist tendencies in both internal policies and consumer-facing product-building practices.

Of course, tech is not alone in this. Reports of workplace sexism, racism, and other types of discrimination are rampant across nearly all industries. These reports are remarkably varied. Some are blatant examples of gender-based harassment or racial bias. Others are more subtle, such as homophobic jokes in work-only chats, promotional giveaways ordered only in men's sizes,

---

[i]   BIPOC stands for Black, Indigenous, and People of Color. Throughout this book, I use this acronym to refer to a group of people who aren't white. See the "Author's Note" for more on this topic.

[ii]   *Latinx* is a gender-neutral term that replaces *Latino* and *Latina* in order to refer inclusively to all people of Latin American descent or culture.

Black people hearing rude comments about their hair, or women partners not being invited on a guys-only coworker outing.

While there's no denying that there's much work left to do, it's not all doom and gloom. Throughout this book, you'll find dozens of stories that show the flip side of this trend, illustrating how allies have made a lasting difference in their organizations. My hope is that many more allies will be inspired to take action in the future and that my inbox will be inundated with success stories.

Why I care

When releasing workforce demographic data, companies often include quotes from white, straight, able-bodied male leaders about the importance of diversity. These men truly believe they're creating meritocracies, that they're treating women and people from other underrepresented groups equitably. Their hearts seem to be in the right place. However, when I look dispassionately at the stories they tell and their lack of progress in actually diversifying their workforces, it becomes clear that many of these leaders are *not* doing everything they can. They're missing opportunities to be authentic allies.

But here's the real kicker: They're also missing out on gaining a competitive advantage. By creating cultures where all people can do their best work and thrive, active allies build businesses that attract the best and brightest talent. The cream of the crop wants to work with and for them, which sounds ideal, yet so few companies commit to diversity in meaningful and lasting ways. So few hit the mark. So few allies make real change possible.

Is it really that hard to act as an ally for underrepresented people in the workplace?

I didn't think so, and after years of observation, I decided to take action. I wanted to learn what meaningful allyship for underrepresented groups in tech might look like. To play what I hoped was at least a small role in making my own industry more diverse and inclusive. To help create workplaces where my friends, my coaching clients, and my daughter (who wanted to be a software engineer since she was little) could do their best work and thrive.

So, in 2014, I started tweeting from an anonymous handle, @betterallies, with the goal of sharing straightforward, simple actions that anyone could take to make their workplace more inclusive. I wanted to demystify allyship and help people in positions of power — particularly men — do their part. I wanted to draw attention to the problem but also offer actionable solutions. Through my tweeting, coupled with responses to my posts and interactions with others working in tech, I amassed many great examples of how allies do act, or should act, in real workplace scenarios. And because they were far too good to let them fade into the Twitter twilight, I compiled them into the first edition of this book. Now — several years and countless ally learnings later — I've updated the text with new information, examples, and recommendations.

This is a guide to help you spot situations in which you can be a better ally to people from all marginalized groups. If you've got the will to support your underrepresented colleagues, you're already ahead of the pack. I'll give you actionable tips so you can transform that will into meaningful change. While my primary audience for the first edition was men in the workplace, I soon learned that this book can be helpful to anyone who is in a position of power. The humbling feedback I received showed me that these lessons and guidelines apply to anyone hoping to build an equitable workplace.

As I wrote each chapter, I did my best to discuss the challenges facing all marginalized groups, with a particular focus on women, BIPOC, people with disabilities, and LGBTQ people.

My personal experience as a white, straight, cisgender[iii], able-bodied woman in tech is bound to influence my perspective, but I've done my best to highlight research and stories that reflect the experiences of other groups in other industries and model what it's like to be an ally to all marginalized groups.

Although it's designed to be read cover to cover, I hope you'll also refer to this book when you want to level up your ally skills and sharpen your competitive advantage around attracting and retaining talent. Use it as a resource when you need to help others course correct during the hiring process, in meetings, at events, or during performance review time. I'd love to see this book on desks everywhere, serving as an accessible and supportive resource for aspiring allies and the underrepresented people they work with and for.

Being an ally is a journey, and it's a journey that I myself am still on. I'm thrilled that you'll be joining me.

[iii]   *Cisgender* means that a person is not transgender; that one's gender identity (or internal sense of self) aligns, according to societal expectations, with the sex assigned at birth.

PART ONE

STARTING
THE
JOURNEY

1

THE ALLY JOURNEY

Allyship is a process. Even seasoned allies with wide open minds are constantly learning and absorbing new information about how to leverage their privilege to support people who are different from them. We all have perspectives that are shaped by our own experiences, so we can't possibly imagine or understand all of the other viewpoints that exist in the world. We must learn about them as we encounter them and adjust our mindsets accordingly. So your first tip for being an ally is to be open to learning, improving, and changing your opinion. And recognize that being an ally is a journey.

This may seem frustrating at first, because it's tempting to want to earn an ally badge and consider oneself to be a lifetime member of the Genuinely Good Human Beings Club. I get it. If this sounds like you, I wrote this book to help you move forward, and I guarantee you'll pick up actionable ideas to be a better ally.

Instead of feeling frustrated that you'll never reach some mythical, fully fledged ally status, remember that we're all learning together. The ally journey is an enlightening and worthwhile one, even though it's a perpetually ongoing one. And

people with privilege who are *truly* dedicated to the empower-
ment of all embrace the fact that doing so means being in a
constant state of learning.

Speaking of which, the time has come to discuss privilege in
both abstract and concrete terms. I promise to keep it
nonjudgmental and encouragement focused!

Let's talk about the "p-word"

Understanding privilege is key to becoming a better ally. At its
core, privilege is a set of unearned benefits given to people who
fit into a specific social group. Due to our race, class, gender,
sexual orientation, language, geographical location, ability,
religion and more, all of us have greater or lesser access to
resources and social power.

People who are marginalized in multiple ways experience
amplified marginalization and drastically reduced privilege. This
is due to intersectionality, the fact that the combination of
someone's identities creates an intersection of overlapping and
compounded oppressions.[9] I appreciate this example by Kittu
Pannu, who wrote about intersectionality in the LGBT community for Impakter:

> One could assume that a black, queer woman would, in
> essence, have a more difficult life experience than a
> heterosexual white male just by virtue of her experiences as a
> woman, compounded with her experience as a black person,
> and topping it off with her queer identity. Her life will be just
> a little harsher, her earning potential just short of the people
> around her, her ability to say with certainty that she gets
> everything she deserves not as strong as a white male's ability.
> She would have to work that much harder to be taken seriously
> in today's heteronormative, white, male-dominated world.[10]

The term *intersectionality* was originally coined by Kimberlé
Crenshaw in her 1989 essay "Mapping the Margins:

Intersectionality, Identity Politics, and Violence against Women of Color," and she explores it further in her excellent TED talk, "The Urgency of Intersectionality."[11] In nearly all cases, being marginalized in multiple ways leads to diminished privilege and increased risk of discrimination and violence.

Now, here's where it gets tricky: Privilege is often invisible to those who have it. This means that many people get defensive when someone points out their privilege. It's tempting to think of privilege as being associated with extreme unearned advantages like having a massive family trust fund or being related to some influential person. Having one's privilege pointed out might feel like the equivalent of being told that one is lazy, lucky, or undeserving of good things — or that one's life has been easy. Many people are quick to respond that they've had their fair share of difficulties and faced down prejudices too.

But doing this means forgetting that privilege is simply a system of advantages granted to all people in a given group. It's a social structure that has become endemic to human cultures. It's not about who you are as an individual as much as it is about which groups you belong to and how those groups are viewed and treated by society. A person isn't privileged because of being a rotten, freeloading bum; They're privileged because they're white or middle-class or cisgender.

Being privileged doesn't mean you've never worked hard, and it doesn't necessarily mean that your life has been easy. Here's a fabulous analogy from Sian Ferguson via the website Everyday Feminism:

> Let's say both you and your friend decide to go cycling. You decide to cycle for the same distance, but you take different routes. You take a route that is a bit bumpy. More often than not, you go down roads that are at a slight decline. It's very hot, but the wind is at [sic] usually at your back. You eventually get to your destination, but you're sunburnt, your legs are aching, you're out of breath, and you have a cramp.

When you eventually meet up with your friend, she says that the ride was awful for her. It was also bumpy. The road she took was at an incline the entire time. She was even more sunburnt than you because she had no sunscreen. At one point, a strong gust of wind blew her over and she hurt her foot. She ran out of water halfway through. When she hears about your route, she remarks that your experience seemed easier than hers.

Does that mean that you didn't cycle to the best of your ability? Does it mean that you didn't face obstacles? Does it mean that you didn't work hard? No. What it means is that you didn't face the obstacles she faced.

Privilege doesn't mean your life is easy or that you didn't work hard. It simply means that you don't have to face the obstacles others have to endure. It means that life is more difficult for those who don't have the systemic privilege you have.[12]

Look at any business segment, and you'll find people who have more privilege than others. In today's tech industry, they tend to be straight, white men. Perhaps they attended highly selective universities such as Stanford, MIT, or an Ivy League school. They may have strong networks of people in similar positions of privilege. They are the majority.

Yet privilege is not limited to straight, white guys.

I'm white, straight, and able-bodied, which means I have a lot of privilege myself. I hold a degree in computer science from Brown University. I'm a published author and a TEDx speaker. Formerly, I was a vice president of engineering at a well-known tech company. Yup. That's a lot of privilege. And my experience is a great reminder that people who are members of systematically oppressed groups (such as women) can still have privilege due to their membership in other groups (such as being white, straight, etc.).

Fifty potential privileges in the workplace

Now for the hard part: Take a moment to examine your own privilege, and reflect on the benefits or obstacles you face at work. Using the list below, quiz yourself by measuring how your privilege compares to your coworkers.

As you review this list, keep a tally. Note any items that surprise you and make you wonder, "Does anyone actually face this challenge?"

1. You are white.
2. You are male.
3. You are straight.
4. You are cisgender (you identify as the gender you were assigned at birth).
5. You're not significantly younger or older than your coworkers.
6. You don't have any disabilities, visible or otherwise.
7. You have a college degree.
8. You attended an elite university.
9. If you're working in the United States, you were born there, or you're a citizen.
10. English is your first language.
11. You don't receive comments about your accent or the way you pronounce certain words.
12. You've never been passed over for a job (or fired from one) based on your gender, race or ethnicity, religion, age, body shape or size, disability, or sexual orientation.
13. You are partnered and feel comfortable speaking openly about your significant other.
14. You're not the primary caregiver for anyone else.
15. You feel welcome at networking opportunities.
16. You aren't asked to do menial tasks that colleagues of another gender or race are asked to do.
17. Others don't routinely assume you're at a lower seniority level than you are.
18. You feel comfortable actively and effectively contributing to meetings you attend.
19. You're rarely interrupted or ignored in meetings.

20. You are confident that if you raise an idea in a meeting, you'll be credited for that idea.
21. Your manager maintains eye contact when speaking to you.
22. You recently received feedback about a technical skill you need to learn.
23. You have spare time to spend learning new job skills or, if you're in tech, working on open source projects.
24. You haven't been told to wait your turn for a promotion or plum project assignment behind an equally qualified peer.
25. You have gotten a job or a promotion with the help of a social, family, or school-related connection.
26. You can talk about political or identity-oriented extracurricular activities without fear of judgment or bias from colleagues.
27. You can observe the holy days in your religious tradition without having to use vacation days.
28. You feel welcome and valued on group projects.
29. You've never been called a "diversity hire."
30. When meeting people at professional events, they assume you're attending in a professional role (versus being the partner of an attendee or that you work in an administrative role).
31. At events, people don't mistake you for a member of the catering staff.
32. You don't receive unwanted sexual advances at work.
33. You haven't had to change teams or companies because of harassment.
34. You feel physically safe at work and at professional events.
35. You feel safe leaving work late at night and going home after evening events.
36. You have stable housing.
37. You're confident that if you were to lose your job, you'd be able to land another one without worrying about paying bills.
38. You can afford to join out-of-office lunches or after-work social activities.

39. You can manage monthly payments on any debt you have.
40. You never have to decide which bills to pay or go without meals because of not being able to afford food.
41. You're not financially supporting a parent, grandparent, sibling, or other extended family members.
42. You have a partner who takes on a large share of household and family responsibilities.
43. You're rarely, if ever, late to work or miss work because of a child's illness or family emergency.
44. You don't have a long career gap on your resume.
45. You've never been arrested, incarcerated, or charged with a criminal offense.
46. People never touch you or your hair without consent.
47. You're comfortable speaking in meetings without worrying someone will find a flaw in your logic and prove you're not qualified to be there.
48. You don't receive abusive comments on social media.
49. You don't remember the last time someone was condescending or overly pedantic when explaining a topic to you.
50. You don't depend on a sponsor, mentor, or any other ally to be respected and taken seriously.

Even if you happen to have all fifty of the above privileges, the intent here is not to make you feel guilty or ashamed. By contrast, the invitation is simply to be aware of your advantages and leverage them empathetically; beating yourself up about them is totally counterproductive.

That said, privilege is often a key ingredient in cultivating professional confidence — confidence that you can leverage your network to get a new job, raise capital for a startup, find a publisher for your book, or score a speaking engagement. Confidence that when you make a killer point at the meeting, others will pay attention. Confidence that people will direct questions to you if you're the expert in the room. Confidence that you're getting paid equitably. Confidence that other attendees at a networking social event will assume you're qualified to be there and not part of the waitstaff. Confidence that people believe you landed your current role because of experience and potential, not solely because you're a woman or a person of color. The list goes on.

Because of my privilege, I know I've received many benefits over my career, and those benefits have empowered me with confidence. I feel ready to use my standing to help foster confidence in others now, and if you are also in a position to do so, I hope you'll join me.

Roles allies can play

It's up to people who hold positions of privilege to be active allies to those with less access and take responsibility for making changes that will help others be successful. Active allies utilize their credibility to create a more inclusive workplace where everyone can thrive, and they find ways to make their privilege work for others.

And wielding privilege as an ally doesn't have to be hard. I've seen allies at all levels take action with simple, everyday efforts that made a difference. Often a big difference! Here are a few roles that allies can choose to play to support colleagues from underrepresented groups in beneficial ways.

The Sponsor

I once worked for a software company that was acquired by a larger company. In the first few months following the acquisition, I noticed something interesting. My new manager, Digby Horner — who had been at the larger company for many years — said things in meetings along the lines of "What I learned from Karen is the following ..."

By doing this, Digby helped me build credibility with my new colleagues. He took action as an ally, using his position of privilege to sponsor me. His shout-outs made a difference and definitely made me feel great.

When an ally takes on the role of the Sponsor, they vocally support the work of colleagues from underrepresented groups in all contexts, but specifically in situations that will help boost those colleagues' standing and reputations.

Other ways to act as a Sponsor:

- Talk about the expertise you see in others, especially during performance calibrations and promotion discussions.
- Recommend people for stretch assignments and learning opportunities.
- Share colleagues' career goals with decision makers.

The Champion

In May 2015, Andrew Grill was a global managing partner at IBM and a speaker at the Online Influence Conference. He was on a panel along with five other men when a woman in the audience posed the obvious question to the all-male lineup: "Where are the women?"

The moderator then asked the panelists to address the topic of gender diversity, and Grill, after sharing some of his thoughts, quickly realized he wasn't the best person to respond. In fact, none of the panelists were. He instead asked the woman who asked the question, Miranda Bishop, to take his place on stage. By stepping aside, Grill made a bold statement in support of gender diversity on stage and championed Bishop at the same time.[13]

Since then, the nonprofit organization GenderAvenger has created a pledge to reduce the frequency of all-male panels at conferences and events. It reads, "I will not serve as a panelist at a public conference when there are no women on the panel." (They also clearly state that transgender women are women.) Anyone can sign the pledge at *www.genderavenger.com*.

Some popular male speakers, such as Jeff Kosseff, a professor at the U.S. Naval Academy, have even added "Won't speak on all-male panels" to their Twitter bios. White women could use a version that says, "Won't speak on all-white panels." (I've done this myself.)

When an ally takes on the role of the Champion, that ally acts similarly to the Sponsor but does so in more public venues. Champions willingly defer to colleagues from underrepresented groups in meetings and in visible, industry-wide events and conferences, sending meaningful messages to large audiences.

Other ways to act as a Champion:

- Direct questions about specific topics to employees with subject-matter expertise instead of answering them yourself.
- Advocate for more women, BIPOC, and members of other underrepresented groups as keynote speakers and panelists.

- If you are asked to keynote or serve in a similar public role and know someone from an underrepresented group who'd be an equally good fit (or better), recommend that person (after asking them first if they'd like to be put forward).

The Amplifier

In a Slack channel for women and nonbinary technical leaders, I met a data engineer who was working at a sixty-person startup. One team inside the company had an unproductive meeting culture that was starting to feel truly toxic. Yelling and interrupting frequently took place at the team's meetings, and women, in particular, felt they couldn't voice their opinions without being shouted over.

One of this engineer's colleagues decided to take action to ensure that the voices of those who weren't shouting would be heard. She introduced communication guidelines for a weekly meeting and saw an immediate improvement. The guidelines included assigning a meeting mediator (team members would take turns in this role), setting clear objectives and an agenda for every meeting, conducting a meeting evaluation by every participant at the end of every meeting, and reminding the members to be respectful and practice active listening. This made it easier for anyone who wasn't comfortable joining the yelling — such as introverts, team members for whom English was a second language, neurodiverse participants, and others — to contribute to important discussions.

When an ally takes on the role of the Amplifier, that ally works to ensure that marginalized voices are both heard and respected. This type of allyship can take many forms, but it is focused on representation within communication.

Other ways to act as an Amplifier:

- When someone proposes a good idea, repeat it, and give them credit. For example: "I agree with Helen's recommendation for improving our customer satisfaction rating."
- Create a code of conduct for meetings and any shared communication medium, including email, chat, Slack, and so forth.
- Invite members of underrepresented groups within your company to speak at staff meetings, write for company-wide newsletters, or take on other highly visible roles.

The Advocate

Early in her career at General Electric, Tanya Spencer caught an important break when Lloyd Trotter invited her to accompany him on a customer call. Trotter was an executive vice president of the company at the time and a founding member of their African American Forum. By including Spencer on this key call, he enabled her to be promoted to her first management position.

"He gave me a chance to get in front of people and to show what I could do," Spencer explained in a GE profile of the African American Forum. She has now worked at GE for more than 25 years and manages the company's Accelerated Leadership Program, an executive development curriculum.[14]

Here's another example. Shortly after she became CEO of YouTube, Susan Wojcicki spoke up about how the tech industry titan Bill Campbell had advocated for her. In an article for *Vanity Fair*, she wrote:

> I learned about an important invitation-only conference convening most of the top leaders in tech and media, yet my name was left off the guest list. Many of the invitees were my peers, meaning that YouTube wouldn't be represented while deals were cut and plans were made. I started to question whether I even belonged at the conference. But rather than let it go, I turned to Bill, someone I knew had a lot of influence and could help fix the situation. He immediately recognized I had a rightful place at the event and within a day he worked his magic and I received my invitation.[15]

When an ally takes on the role of the Advocate, they use their power and influence to bring peers from underrepresented groups into highly exclusive circles. The Advocate recognizes and addresses unjust omissions, holding their peers accountable for including qualified colleagues of all genders, races, abilities, ages, body shapes and sizes, religions, and sexual orientations.

Other ways to act as an Advocate:

- Look closely at the invite list for events, strategic planning meetings, dinners with key partners, and other career-building opportunities. If you see someone from a marginalized group missing, advocate for them to be invited.
- Offer to introduce colleagues from underrepresented groups to influential people in your network.
- Ask someone from an underrepresented group to be a coauthor or collaborator on a proposal or conference submission.

The Scholar

I'm a member of the Women's CLUB of Silicon Valley, a nonprofit leadership incubator for women. Many of our events are open to guests, who come to hear the speakers and participate in our workshops. Most guests are women, so it stood out when a male guest started attending our events. I asked one of my friends who he was, and she told me he was a former colleague who wanted to better understand the challenges women face in the workplace. He spent many evenings at our events, listening and absorbing information about the issues we discussed so he could be a better ally.

When an ally takes on the role of the Scholar, that ally seeks to learn as much as possible about the challenges and prejudices faced by colleagues from marginalized groups. It's important to note that Scholars never insert their own opinions, experiences, or ideas, but instead simply listen and learn. They also don't expect marginalized people to provide links to research proving that bias exists or to summaries of best practices. Scholars do their own research to seek out relevant information.

Other ways to act as a Scholar:

- Investigate and read publications, podcasts, or social media by and about underrepresented groups within your industry.
- Ask coworkers from marginalized groups about their experience working in your organization.
- If your organization or industry has specific discussion forums or Slack channels for members of under-represented groups, ask if they'd be comfortable letting

you sit in to observe. Asking is essential: Your presence may cause members to censor themselves, so be sure to check in before showing up.

The Upstander

I remember being impressed by Lisa, a white software engineer who stepped outside of her comfort zone to be an ally. When asked to name her "spirit animal" as part of a team-building exercise, Lisa spoke up. She wasn't comfortable taking part in an exercise that appropriated Native American spiritual traditions.

When an ally takes on the role of the Upstander, that ally acts as the *opposite* of a bystander. The Upstander is someone who sees wrongdoing and acts to combat it. This person pushes back on offensive comments or jokes, even if no one within earshot might be offended or hurt.

Other ways to act as an Upstander:

- Always speak up if you witness behavior or speech that is degrading or offensive. Explain your stance so everyone is clear about why you are raising the issue.
- In meetings, shut down off-topic questions that are asked only to test the presenter.
- Take action if you see anyone being bullied or harassed. Simply insert yourself into a conversation with a comment like, "Hi! What are you folks discussing?" and then check in with the victim privately. Ask if they are okay and if they want you to say something.

The Confidant

A couple of years ago, I spoke with Emily, a college-aged intern who told me about a one-on-one meeting with her mentor. When he asked what she wanted to do post-graduation, Emily emphasized that her top priority was to find an inclusive work environment. When he asked why, she shared her experience working at a previous internship. Her manager there wouldn't make eye contact with her, and he directed all technical questions about her project to her coding partner, a male intern. The mentor listened to Emily, incredulous at first but then quickly supportive. Although he had heard rumors, he hadn't truly believed things like this happened until she shared this experience with him. By listening and believing, he both supported his mentee and validated her experience in the tech industry.

When an ally takes on the role of the Confidant, that ally creates a safe space for members of underrepresented groups to express their fears, frustrations, and needs. Simply listening to their stories and trusting that they're being truthful creates a protective layer of support.

Other ways to act as a Confidant:

- Believe others' experiences. Don't assume something couldn't happen just because you haven't personally experienced it.
- Listen and ask questions when someone describes an experience you haven't had. Don't jump in with your personal stories.

- If you are a manager, hold regular "office hours" and encourage all of your team members to speak with you about issues that are troubling them.

The perfectly imperfect ally

In this chapter, I've shared just a few examples of how people with privilege have acted as allies in specific roles. It's important to note that, while these people all chose to use their power to support others, they're humans and therefore not perfect. And they don't need to be.

It can be hard to have conversations about race, especially if you haven't experienced the racial inequity and systemic oppression that other people face. Or to discuss gender inequity as a man in a male-dominated industry. You may be concerned you'll make a mistake. That you might say the wrong thing. Or act in a way that's not helpful and possibly even hurtful. It can be a lot easier to pull back from these conversations and become simply a bystander.

But here's the thing. The world needs more upstanders, especially now with the growing concern about the treatment of Black people in America. We need more people who see wrong-doing and take action. People who push for change. People who aren't comfortable with the status quo, even though they may have benefited from it.

We also need people who are okay making mistakes along the way. Being an ally is a journey, and one that I am on myself. With each mistake I make, I have an opportunity to learn and do things differently. I have the opportunity to have a greater impact. But this happens only if I put in the effort.

In an article titled "Get it wrong for me: What I need from allies," Megan Carpenter of Microsoft wrote:

I want a bunch of people who are interested in becoming allies to me to get it wrong. Because I promise, you will get it wrong, likely more than once. But please get it wrong, for me. Be wrong on my behalf. Try stuff, learn stuff, make attempts, and fail. Embrace the discomfort of not knowing, of not being certain, of not understanding, and then be motivated enough to learn and get better. I will give you grace if you give me effort.[16]

Brené Brown is of the same mind. In *Dare to Lead*, she wrote,

People are opting out of vital conversations about diversity and inclusivity because they fear looking wrong, saying something wrong, or being wrong. Choosing our own comfort over hard conversations is the epitome of privilege, and it corrodes trust and moves us away from meaningful and lasting change.[17]

Let's all put in the effort and be okay with making mistakes. Because the best allies are willing to make mistakes and keep trying. They acknowledge when they're wrong or could do better, and they correct their course. They resist getting defensive and insisting that they're already doing enough. They listen and learn. They iterate.

Fortunately, there are many opportunities in every workplace to listen, learn, and take action as allies. It's something anyone can do. In the coming chapters, we'll explore how to spot situations where you can be a better ally and everyday actions that will make a difference.

Actions for Better Allies:
Understand Your Privilege and Use It for Good

An important part of allyship is being open to learning, improving, and taking action.

- Review the list of fifty potential privileges in the workplace that was included in this chapter. How many apply to you?
- Identify at least one way you can be a better ally, using the archetypes in this chapter.
- Understand that being an ally is a journey. We all make mistakes. Don't let that hold you back from taking action. Don't opt out.

KNIGHTS VERSUS ALLIES

A few years ago, I published an article on *www.opensource.com* about why I started Better Allies.[18] Given the website's large reader base and boatload of followers on Twitter, I knew it would help increase awareness of my initiative. I also had a feeling it might generate some criticism. As Jason van Gumster wrote previously to the open source community, "Haters are an inevitable part of sharing your work."[19]

On publication day, I mentally prepared myself; hoping for support, yet ready to handle any backlash. When I checked Twitter early in the morning, I saw lots of great comments and retweets of the article. Phew!

Next came responses from some folks who disagreed, saying things like, "I'm here to earn my paycheck, not take care of other people." (Expletives removed. Several of these folks needed to both vent *and* swear.) And there were a handful of pointed jabs calling me a creep and instructing me to eff off. Nothing I couldn't handle.

But then ... a surprise. I saw a few critical tweets that made me think deeply about my work on Better Allies and how it might be perceived. These tweets were from women who completely dismissed the need for allies. Women who didn't want to be placed in a homogeneous group that couldn't speak for themselves. Women who bristled at the implied need for knights to ride in on horses and save them from toxic workplace cultures.

I'd expected to hear from some haters, but to learn from them? That caught me off guard.

It also got me thinking about how actions that were meant to be supportive could feel patronizing. I realized that good intentions were never going to be enough. Real allies needed to carefully consider the repercussions of their actions, too. These tweets also helped me refine my own goals: I don't want to be a knight riding in to save the day. I don't want to view anyone who is underrepresented as a virtual damsel in distress. I don't want to serve as anyone's protector. No. Never. Instead, I want to transform current workplace cultures into ones where everyone can thrive. I want to question the norms that have allowed folks like me to get ahead, encourage productive conversation around prejudices, and take everyday actions to support members of marginalized groups. And I want to bring others along on this journey.

Tech policy expert and community organizer Corey Ponder wrote about coming to the same realization in an article titled, "Allyship is Not the Hero's Journey."

> Underserved and underrepresented communities aren't looking for — nor do they need — heroes or last-minute miracles. Allyship isn't about being a savior. Allyship is the journey of the trusted sidekick. And that is because sidekicks do three things very well —
> 1. They show up for everyday moments.
> 2. They are willing to confront ugly truths, especially about themselves.
> 3. They use their special abilities to help the protagonist achieve their goals.

… When we show up as trusted sidekicks, we create a permissive environment that allows people to be their most authentic and productive selves. We empower people to fight for and build the world they want to see. And that is the true journey of an ally.[20]

Like Ponder, I know that part of that journey will involve teaching myself and others how to translate our heartfelt intentions into meaningful, constructive actions — and avoid being inadvertently condescending or patronizing.

How to tell a knight from an ally

So, what are the differences between ally actions and knight actions? I believe it comes down to two things: mindset and systemic change. Allies take action to empower individuals, not to rescue them or put themselves in the spotlight. Allies also seek to create systemic change, not one-off savior moves. Here are some examples.

Scenario 1

Imagine you are part of a hiring committee, and you realize the group is measuring candidates inconsistently. Group members are using subjective criteria that treat the one candidate from an underrepresented group less favorably than the rest of the pool. Let's call that candidate Willie.

The group's biased objections to Willie might sound like, "I just didn't click with him. I can't quite put my finger on it." Or, "I don't think I'd feel comfortable putting him in front of customers." Or perhaps someone might say, "Willie doesn't have the four to six years of coding experience listed in the job description," even though other candidates who also lacked that experience were given a thumbs-up.

A knight would push back to give Willie a better chance, trying to save him from being eliminated from the hiring process. The knight might say, "I think Willie can do the job. In fact, I'll personally mentor him to help him be successful." This might result in a positive outcome for one marginalized person, but it is less likely to have a lasting impact on hiring policies.

By contrast, an ally would push back on this specific decision *and* seek systemic change so that the situation would not occur again. For example, the ally might say, "Folks, I'll personally mentor Willie if we hire him, but let's step back. I'm concerned we're not consistently evaluating our candidates. Let's identify objective criteria that we can use to measure everyone. Moving forward, I'd like to discuss how we can make this a best practice for all hiring committees."

Scenario 2

Imagine noticing a person being interrupted in a meeting. Let's call her Mei. She's tried to make her point a few times, but someone always cuts her off.

A knight might step in to save her by saying, "I think Mei was making a good point. Let me summarize." If the knight has substantially more privilege than Mei, it might feel appropriate to both acknowledge her idea and put it into their own words. After all, that would mean using their power to highlight her talent. However, it might also result in listeners remembering the knight's recap more clearly than Mei's initial explanation and crediting the knight with the idea.

An ally would redirect the conversation back to Mei's capable hands with, "I'd like to get back to what Mei was saying." An ally would do this consistently, any time they witnessed someone being talked over. The ally could also institute a no-interruption rule for future meetings or an overall code of conduct that creates a respectful environment for all speakers. (More on this in Chapter 5.)

Scenario 3

Say one of your direct reports is a nonbinary individual, and you've had several conversations about the restroom signage on your floor. You both agree that it's time to update the labels, and since your department takes up the whole floor, you have the power to spearhead some changes.

A knight might tape "All Gender" signs to the restroom doors and proudly make an announcement to the department via email.

In addition to getting temporary signs up ASAP, an ally would open a conversation with company leadership about restroom policies, then work with the facilities team to review restrooms throughout the building and determine a longer-term solution. (Many thanks to my friend Jeannie Gainsburg and her book *The Savvy Ally: A Guide for Becoming a Skilled LGBTQ+ Advocate* for this example.)

Scenario 4

I recently coached a client, Amanda, who led a large department of highly skilled tech workers. While working on performance rankings, she noticed that one woman's salary was significantly lower than that of her male peers.

Acting as a knight would have been the easiest route for Amanda to take. With one quick update to a spreadsheet, she could have adjusted that employee's salary. She could have fixed the inequity and felt good about treating that woman more fairly. But Amanda recognized that she could use her position and privilege to do more, to push beyond helping just one person.

Instead, Amanda led an initiative to perform a salary review by gender, not just for her department but for her company as a whole. It was a lot more work, but it led to changes that supported the entire employee base. She also ensured that the compensation processes would treat new hires and existing employees fairly and equitably; it created lasting, systemic change.

Amanda's initiative even uncovered some unexpected data: In addition to identifying women who were underpaid, she found a handful of men whose salaries were significantly lower than the salaries of their peers. Because her goal was to treat everyone equitably and not just identify women who were underpaid, she recommended compensation audits for the departments where those discrepancies were found. Now that's what I call allyship.

Scenario 5

In workplaces around the world, there are many leaders who act as Sponsors, Champions, and Advocates. They recommend individuals for stretch assignments. They talk about others' accomplishments to highlight the impact they're making on the business. They use their organizational clout to open doors.

Sheree Atcheson, now the global director of diversity, equity & inclusion at Peakon, told me how a sponsor helped her to grow her career. He actively opted out of opportunities, passing them along to her instead. He mentioned her in meetings and ensured that clients had her contact info so they can follow up with her directly. In her words, "He enabled me to create stronger business connections."

When Atcheson told me about her sponsor, I initially thought, "What a good guy." But I also wondered if he was truly an ally or more of a knight, setting her up for success to "save" her from being stuck at a certain level of her career.

Atcheson quickly disagreed. She told me that he also worked to change the culture so that other leaders acted as sponsors, passing along opportunities. Plus, she pointed out that he actively gave her constructive feedback, helping her to grow and be less dependent on him to open career doors on her behalf.

Scenario 6

Years ago, I remember sitting in a conference room, waiting for my manager to arrive for a weekly staff meeting. One of my colleagues, John, asked me if I was flying to the off-site meeting that night or the next day. I replied with a surprised, "What are you talking about?" John told me that our CEO was hosting a three-day meeting at his vacation compound in Canada and had invited all the vice presidents. Or so John thought. Clearly, I hadn't made the list.

Acting as a knight, John could have talked to the CEO's assistant and explained why I should be extended a last-minute invitation.

A better action would have been to ask how the invite list was formed, suggest ways to make sure that the process going forward would be fair and unbiased, and help ensure that future meetings would be handled more equitably.

Unfortunately, I don't think John did either of these things. Not only did I not receive a last-minute invitation to that year's off-site meeting, I also wasn't invited the following year either. Nor was another female vice president. To this day, we fondly call each other "chopped liver" and "pond scum" in a show of solidarity.

How to screen your actions

Worried that your good intentions may lead to knight-like behaviors? Use this rubric to screen your actions and responses for savior-style thinking:

- What do I hope to accomplish by doing this?
- How many people will this help?
- How will my action/response change ingrained behaviors within my company?

- If I do/say this, will it matter to anyone a year from now? Five years from now?
- Will this action create equality or equity? Will it remove barriers?

EQUALITY   **EQUITY**

Image courtesy of Paul Kuttner of *www.culturalorganizing.org* [21]

There will be times when catalyzing large-scale change within your company or industry will feel impossible, and that's just fine. Take action in the moment, for a single person, yet strive to have a lasting impact. The goal is to do more and do better as often as you can. Perfection may be impossible, but improvement is well within reach. And on that note ...

Allies do what's right, not what's easy

Often, the knight move is the simplest and the easiest course. It can be tempting to take action quickly so you can feel like you're having a real, measurable impact right away. Let's face it: The working world is fast-paced, and our days are often filled with competing priorities. Plus, there are never enough hours in the day. Why bother taking on a big initiative to drive systemic change when I can get something done, check it off my list, and know I helped at least one person?

Because it matters. Because the larger, systemic changes will help shift the ratios in favor of all those who are marginalized under the current systems. Because doing what's right instead of what's easy will lead to a more inclusive workplace where everyone can thrive — and that will result in more innovation, better solutions for customers, and better business results.

In business, we don't need knights in shining armor, but we do need allies to take action and be ambassadors for change. How will you make sure you're acting as an ally, not a knight? What systemic changes can you institute to create more inclusive workplace cultures — not just for a marginalized individual or two, but for all?

Actions for Better Allies:
Be an Ambassador for Change

Helping individuals is laudable, but the responsibility of allies is to take actions that will have lasting, beneficial effects on systems (as often as possible).

- When lending a hand to a single person, step back to look for systemic changes that will benefit many employees.
- Suggest new processes that will change ingrained behaviors and create a more inclusive culture.
- Pay attention to your motivations: Focus on what will authentically support marginalized people over the long-term, rather than what will make you feel or look good.

3

LISTENING AND LEARNING

No matter how hard you try or how often you immerse yourself in perspectives other than your own, *you will never be a perfect ally.* None of us will! It's simply not possible to know everything or anticipate the needs and expectations of everyone in our companies or industries. Although this may seem frustrating and overwhelming on the surface, I encourage you to employ an age-old, perception-shifting trick: Consider it a challenge instead — a challenge to be curious, to listen and be open-minded, and to iterate as you learn.

We cannot know everything, but we *can* be open to constant learning. We cannot anticipate the needs and expectations of everyone, but we *can* listen when the people around us voice those needs and expectations. We can be respectfully inquisitive, eager to assimilate new information, and ready to alter our ideas and behaviors as needed. Valuable allies ask questions instead of making statements. Valuable allies are agile and willing to reevaluate "the way things are done around here." Valuable allies are on a journey, learning as they go.

What does that mean in action? For starters, it means learning how to discuss discrimination that you have never experienced with someone who experiences it on a regular basis.

How to open the door to learning

There are no two ways about it: Broaching subjects like sexism, racism, harassment, and discrimination in the workplace is hard. These are tough and touchy topics, and many potential allies worry that simply bringing them up may cause rifts. Or that they may say the wrong thing and make the situation worse. This is understandable and worth acknowledging.

However, it is *not* an acceptable excuse for inaction. Remember that true allies take responsibility for learning to do what's right instead of falling back on what's easy. Sparking meaningful change requires pushing past our own fears and being willing to get vulnerable. And even make a few mistakes.

What does that vulnerability look like in the field? Here's a great example: On Twitter, I received a direct message from Dave, who had recently taken a leadership role in the allies group at his tech company. He told me he was struggling to figure out where to start and wondered if I had any suggestions.

I asked, "Do you have specific goals for the group? Have you defined success metrics?"

Well, it turns out that was the heart of the issue. Dave was looking for ideas for good goals, with a focus on educating people on how to be allies, but he was worried about looking like the prototypical white guy telling people about other groups' experiences. He wanted to lead and support and create change, but he didn't want to be cast as an indiscriminate mansplainer.

I recommended he turn it around and ask the company's women-in-tech group and other employee resource groups about some of their biggest challenges. From there, he could facilitate a cross-group brainstorming session on how allies could help. For example, those groups might report that they don't have equitable access to mentoring, aren't asked to give presentations at company meetings, aren't invited to attend key customer events, or aren't informed about rotation or stretch assignments. Armed with these insights, Dave could craft a strategy for his allies group to address the areas of need, as well as metrics to measure success.

In other words, he could listen and learn. Instead of guessing what colleagues from underrepresented groups might need and launching initiatives based on conjecture, he was better served to ask these colleagues *exactly how they wanted to be helped.*

This approach is key to effective allyship, both within the workplace and outside of it. It's inappropriate for allies to assume that they know what's best for an underrepresented group and that it's potentially harmful to take action on those assumptions. It's far better for people in positions of power and/or privilege to open productive discussions with people from underrepresented groups about how they'd like to be supported by allies. If this is you, here are some best practices.

Ask to ask. You'd like to talk with a colleague about their challenges, and that's great! But as someone in a position of privilege, you should ask if your colleague is comfortable and willing to discuss their experiences. Don't assume that they're just waiting to be plied with questions. Ask if they'd be open to a dialogue around discrimination or bias, and *then* dig into your specific questions on the topic. This is especially important when it comes to issues of race. Many well-meaning white people ask their Black friends and colleagues to explain cultural and historical contexts or make them feel like they must speak on behalf of all Black people. This is draining and exhausting. So before you dive into your questions, ask to ask.

Acknowledge your fears. Consider opening a dialogue by owning up to your worries about the topic. When you approach a discussion about discrimination by saying, "I'm hoping to get your insights, but am a little concerned about putting my foot in my mouth," you pave the way for honesty. In fact, if you're in a leadership position and choose to be sincere about your imperfections, doubts, and mistakes, you automatically make it safer for others to voice their own feelings and fears.[22]

Be open and respectful. This may seem obvious, but in the context of discrimination discussions, "being open and respectful" may take on some less-than-obvious implications. If you are approaching a member of a marginalized group with questions about their experiences in the workplace, you must be prepared to acknowledge and accept any information they impart. Broadcasting respect means trusting the speaker to share their truth.

For instance, if a Black woman tells you, "My supervisor is far more critical of my grammar than she is of my white colleagues'," and you say, "Oh, that can't be true! Your supervisor is a great leader," you are invalidating and dismissing her perspective. Similarly, as you hear about biased behavior, you may be tempted to respond with a positive spin, such as, "I don't think they meant to offend you." Even if your own experience runs counter to what she's telling you, it's your job as an ally to listen and respect her viewpoint. Approaching dialogue from a respectful place helps diffuse tension and create space for meaningful sharing.[23]

Don't get defensive. As you hear about someone else's experience, you may identify things you could have, or should have, done differently to support them directly or to create a more inclusive culture. You may also find yourself getting defensive, which is understandable. Focus on why you are having this conversation (to listen and learn) as opposed to making excuses for your own behavior. (More on this in the next section.)

Apologize. If you realize you made a mistake, don't double down on your stance. Instead, share a heartfelt apology and discuss how you can do better.

Again, these discussions won't be easy, but they are vital to embracing constructive allyship. Dr. Gwendolyn Keita, executive director of the American Psychological Association's Public Interest Directorate, asserts that addressing bias head-on will become increasingly important over time:

> Human survival may be the most fundamental benefit of eliminating discrimination. That we fear and recoil from those who are different than we are is unfortunate and potentially dangerous. A lack of diversity, perpetuated by discrimination, makes our society weaker. Diversity breeds creative thinking, democratic communities and innovation. Diversity in higher education makes better citizens and results in a more vibrant and prosperous society that benefits everyone. Productive, meaningful dialogues can help contribute significantly to awareness of these important truths.[24]

How to learn without getting defensive

Opening the door to learning about inequity in our workplaces means that some unexpected feedback may flow through. Asking members of underrepresented groups to share their experiences often leads to candid insights about how people with privilege act and speak, which can cause hackles to rise.

As discussed in Chapter 1, when people who are reminded of their privilege get defensive about it, they are acting in a deeply counterproductive way. Pushing back against statements about one's own privilege is one of the quickest ways to shut down communication.

Before I started paying attention to my own privilege, I have to admit I fell into this trap. Years ago, I remember my reaction when hearing someone say, "It's hard for me to get ahead in my career because I don't have a degree from a name-brand university." I found myself thinking, "Well, sure, I went to an Ivy League school, but I did the work to get accepted, took out loans and held a campus job to pay for it, and it wasn't exactly easy to graduate. I worked hard! And now I work just as hard to get ahead in my career." Fortunately, I didn't say any of that out loud. If I had, I bet the conversation would have ended right there.

To be an ally, I have to graciously accept that I have privilege instead of getting defensive. I have to receive feedback about my shortcomings *and* work to assimilate the suggestions I'm given. An essential component of learning is a willingness to change and improve, so I strive to cultivate that within myself, and I invite all others striving to be effective allies to do the same. Wondering how? Here are a few ideas.

Embrace your inherent bias. No one is entirely free of prejudice, myself included. It's a tough pill to swallow, but we need to accept that we're all biased due to our own experiences and perspectives. Entertainment executive Nikki Levy shared a story with The Muse that perfectly illustrates a common bias related to appearance.

> I've had to come out at every job I've ever had because I look so "straight." I am engaged. I wear a ring. When you want to know things like how we met, ask, "How did you meet your partner?" as opposed to, "How did you meet him?" I can't tell you the number of times I've been apologized to because of their assumptions about my non-existent husband.[25]

Our biases don't make us evil, or hypocritical, or useless in the fight against inequity in the workplace. They just make us human. But if we deny our inherent biases, we are contributing to systematized inequity on subtle but important levels. And clinging to the idea that we are bias-free prevents us from receiving tough feedback and learning from it.

Know your counternarratives. On a related note, it's incredibly helpful to know which themes consistently emerge in conversations about gender, race, and other types of discrimination that take place between people with varying amounts of privilege and oppression. If you know the common arguments, you can both understand your own biases and be on alert for biases in those around you.

The Opportunity Agenda, a social justice communication lab, highlights the following common counternarratives. Although they're framed in terms of racism, they could be applied to sexism, ableism, heterosexism, and other oppressions as well.

- Racism is "largely" over or dying out over time.
- People of color are obsessed with race.
- Alleging discrimination is itself racist and divisive.
- Claiming discrimination is "playing the race card," opportunistic, hypocritical demagoguery.
- Civil rights are a crutch for those who lack merit or drive.
- Racism will always be with us, so it's a waste of time to talk about it.[26]

As Chad Loder, an information security leader, shared with me, "I tell white men: Don't go into a conversation to prove a point about gender or race. Instead, ask questions, get people to share their experience, and listen."

Focus on action and improvement. Hearing that you are (or a group you belong to is) doing something wrong is never fun, but without constructive feedback, we can never improve. Being an ally means making our workplaces more inclusive and equitable, and that includes changing our own behaviors as needed. If a colleague from an underrepresented group says you constantly interrupt them in meetings, try to set your feelings aside and focus on the action you can take to rectify the situation. What's important here is making change that will create positive ripples into the future.

Why is this important? Because our ability to accept and absorb criticism and feedback has an immeasurable impact on our colleagues from marginalized groups. Robin DiAngelo, author of *White Fragility: Why It's So Hard for White People to Talk about Racism*, is also a facilitator of trainings on racism. In an article for Medium, she shared the following anecdote:

> In my workshops, I often ask people of color, "How often have you given white people feedback on our unaware yet inevitable racism? How often has that gone well for you?" Eye rolling, head shaking, and outright laughter follow, along with the consensus of rarely, if ever. I then ask, "What would it be like if you could simply give us feedback, have us graciously receive it, reflect, and work to change the behavior?" Recently, a man of color sighed and said, "It would be revolutionary." I ask my fellow whites to consider the profundity of that response. It would be revolutionary if we could receive, reflect, and work to change the behavior.[27]

It's easy to get defensive. Especially if we are white because — as DiAngelo points out in her book — white people have been conditioned to believe that being white is the equivalent to being "neutral." When someone points out that whiteness or the embedded mechanisms of white supremacy are the sources of widespread racial injustice and suffering, a common white response is to feel personally affronted. Having never thought of "whiteness" as a concept at all, white people are caught off guard and resist the idea that they're part of a large and harmful racial force. This is classic white fragility; discomfort and defensiveness on the part of a white person when confronted by information about racial inequality and injustice.

In her podcast episode titled "Brené on Shame and Accountability," Brené Brown implores white people to combat knee-jerk white fragility with understanding. "Those of us who are white and trying to do anti-racism work ... need to understand the difference between being held accountable for racism and experiencing shame as a result of that accountability, and how that's different than being shamed for being a racist," Brown says. "These are two different things."[28]

It can be hard to do in the moment, but it becomes easier when white allies remain actively open to difficult feedback. It becomes *exponentially* easier when white allies commit to doing the work to learn about the history and breadth of racism in our country and are willing to acknowledge our role in it. It's our job to listen and learn, even when both feel uncomfortable. Only after that can we move ourselves toward meaningful action.

As Maya Angelou wisely said, "Do the best you can until you know better. Then when you know better, do better."[29]

A guide to red-flag language

Being an ally requires learning about your own ingrained prejudices, but it also requires helping those around us acknowledge theirs. At the risk of entering broken-record territory, *none of us is bias-free,* and yet many of us have no idea which biases we exhibit. Furthermore, many people have no idea that certain phrases or assertions reflect personal prejudices.

The following is an abbreviated list of language that should raise red flags for allies. In other words, when you hear any of these phrases, pay attention and be ready to take action.

Red-Flag Phrases

The candidate wouldn't be a culture fit.

The candidate doesn't have that qualification (when discussing something not on the job description but that more privileged candidates meet).

They wouldn't want this role because of the travel.

I'd like to see them prove they're capable before promoting them (when discussing some responsibility that they've previously had).

I don't want to lower the bar.

There's not enough pipeline to hire more women or BIPOC.

They are so articulate (when talking about a Black coworker).

Annie, can you take notes? (More on this one in Chapter 7.)

I'm not racist/sexist/homophobic, but …

Well, we're different (when hearing about workplace challenges faced by underrepresented groups).

I've never seen the kind of harassment that they just reported, so I don't think it could happen here.

I'm sure they didn't mean to offend anyone.

That last one is a doozy. It can be hard for allies to accept that intentions aren't enough and that words can still be harmful even when spoken in good faith. Let's dive a little deeper into that concept.

How "assuming positive intent" behaves in the wild

It's fairly common for codes of conduct to include a statement about "assuming positive intent" when interacting with others. This mandate is an attempt to curb unproductive conflict and remind participants that everyone involved is trying their best. It's an idea that comes from a good place, but can unwittingly quash the perspectives of people from underrepresented groups.

Annalee Flower Horne, co-editor at *The Bias*, a website dedicated to diversity and inclusion in tech spaces, explained this issue clearly, saying:

> The harm is that telling people to "assume good intent" is a sign that if they come to you with a concern, you will minimize their feelings, police their reactions, and question their perceptions. It tells marginalized people that you don't see codes of conduct as tools to address systemic discrimination, but as tools to manage personal conflicts without taking power differences into account. Telling people to "assume good intent" sends a message about whose feelings you plan to center when an issue arises in your community.[30]

In essence, including "assume positive intent" in a code of conduct gives careless or ignorant participants a get-out-of-jail-free card; they can say racist or sexist or otherwise inappropriate and harmful things and just claim that they "didn't mean to be offensive" — that their intent was to learn more, or give an innocuous compliment, or point out something that *seemed* harmless.

This approach also puts people from marginalized groups in the position of "breaking the rules" if they see discriminatory behavior and choose to call it out. They're not "assuming positive intent" when they object; they're seen as being "disruptive," "angry," or "overly negative." And when Black people or other people of color "break the rules," they face much harsher social repercussions than their white counterparts. See how this can cause inherent toxicity?

The mandate to assume positive intent seeps out beyond codes of conduct, too. It can become a blanket excuse for inappropriate workplace behavior of all kinds.

Imagine a white male supervisor who has a Latina assistant. They have a solid relationship overall, but nearly every day he comments on her outfit. His comments are positive, generally along the lines of "You look gorgeous today!" or "You look great in turquoise. Latinas aren't afraid of bright colors, are they?" His intent may be to boost her confidence in her appearance, but the net effect is that she feels objectified. If his comments include references to her hair, her curves, or how her choices reflect her culture, she may also feel ethnically pigeonholed.

Now imagine her choices. She can go to HR and say that her boss's daily compliments make her feel uncomfortable, but she risks being scolded for failing to "assume positive intent." Lodging her complaint may ruin her relationship with her supervisor forever and even make her a pariah among her coworkers. Her other option is to grit her teeth and endure his observations, gradually becoming more frustrated with his well-meaning behavior. She remains miserable, and her boss continues behaving in inappropriate and offensive ways without knowing he's doing anything wrong.

Intent is not valueless, especially because plenty of people do racist and sexist things with full knowledge of how their actions will be received. That said, positive intent is not a justification for discrimination or ignorance. Insisting that colleagues "assume positive intent" can create damaging conditions in the workplace. So instead, let's work to set expectations around *demonstrating* positive intent through respectful action.

Combating the bystander effect as an ally

Although this chapter is all about listening and learning, listening is not enough when we see biased, offensive, or inappropriate behavior. Listening and keeping quiet doesn't make us neutral; It makes us complicit.

Does coming forward and objecting feel uncomfortable? For many of us, the answer is a resounding, "Heck yes." But this discomfort is nothing compared to how it feels for the person whose racial group is being joked about. Or the colleague who is forced to endure constant commentary about her appearance. Or the coworker who is being excluded due to a disability. The discomfort of allies pales in comparison to what people from marginalized groups are forced to live through on a daily basis.

Let's explore a few situations where allies could have moved from *bystanders* to *upstanders*.

Situation 1

In July 2020, I spoke on a panel along with Minda Harts, bestselling author of *The Memo: What Women of Color Need to Know to Secure a Seat at the Table*. After introductions and a general discussion, Harts described some real-life scenarios and asked me how someone could have acted as a success partner in each. (As Harts explains in her book, she prefers "success partner" to "ally." She's tired of the word "ally" because of people who wear the ally badge without doing anything to earn it.)

For one of those scenarios, Harts suggested a conversation among three people in which a Black coworker is discussing why Black Lives Matter. Suddenly, a white coworker chimes in with "All Lives Matter." She centers the conversation on herself and starts describing how all women have it bad.

What happened: The white colleague completely shut down the conversation, the Black colleague walked away feeling unheard and disrespected, and the bystander colleague was too overwhelmed to speak up.

What should have happened: I suggested that the bystander colleague could employ one of my favorite techniques: Seek common ground and then educate. Here's what that might look like. "I agree women have it bad in the workplace, and there have been times I've felt like saying All Lives Matter. But I've since learned that Black Lives Matter doesn't mean Black lives are more important than others. Instead, it means that because Black lives are undervalued, we need to focus on fixing that." Then the bystander (now an upstander) would hand the proverbial mic over to their Black colleague with a quick "So, let's get back to what Raymond was saying."

Situation 2

Harts shared another example that illustrates how hurtful it can be when a potential ally chooses to be a bystander. When she was twenty-four years old, she was riding in a car with her manager and another colleague. It was summer, and Harts was wearing bright orange nail polish. Her manager said, "You people love your bright colors,"[31] then laughed and joked about Black people's color preferences with the other colleague for several minutes.

What happened: The colleague said nothing and laughed along with the manager.

What should have happened: When hearing a racist or offensive comment, an ally can speak up with, "I don't get it. Why is that so funny?" or "What makes you say that?" This approach gets the person to confront their bias, forcing them to dig into their reasoning aloud. They may decide it's not worth explaining and drop the topic quickly.

I asked Harts how she would have felt if her colleague in the car had spoken up that day and asked the manager to explain himself. She said it would have made all the difference in the world.

Situation 3

A few years back, I met with Pete, an engineering leader in San Francisco, to discuss how to improve diversity in his research lab. As I asked about the office culture and what they did for fun as a team, Pete had a mini a-ha moment. He said, "So, last week, a few guys went to a strip club for lunch. That's probably not a best practice?"

What happened: Pete didn't push back when he heard about the lunchtime outing.

What should have happened: Pete could have pointed out that not everyone feels comfortable going to a strip club and then recommended a few other lunchtime spots where the entire team could hang out together.

Being an upstander

As an ally, how can you equip yourself to confront discrimination and inappropriate behavior when you see it? Here are some ideas. (The first four come from the Teaching Tolerance website.[32])

Be ready. Start to think of yourself as an Upstander, someone who can and does speak up. Visualize yourself seeing injustice and taking action. Consider queuing up some open-ended responses like "What makes you feel that way?" or "Why do you say that?" Another idea is a simple "We don't do that here."

Verbalize what you're seeing. Because many people have no idea that they're biased, sometimes just reflecting back at them jars them into understanding. Point out behavior or language bluntly, but avoid accusations. Try this: "Andy, what I hear you saying is that all gay men are overly dramatic." Or "Susan, you're classifying an entire gender/ethnicity/group in a derogatory way. Is that what you mean to say?"

Compare to past behavior. Letting someone know they're doing something out of character is a great way to alert them to inappropriate behavior. Try appealing to their better instincts with something like "Jim, I've always thought of you as a fair-minded person. I'm shocked to hear you say something that sounds so bigoted."

Set boundaries. You may not be able to change someone's mind, but you can set limits to their behavior when they're around you. Try "Don't tell racist jokes in my presence anymore." Or "I don't tolerate homophobic remarks in my work space. Please respect my wishes."

Create a template. While one-to-one conversations are powerful, you can also get creative. Steve Andersen, who is vice president of services at Exponent Partners, pointed out that some upstander behavior can be handled electronically. He tweeted:[33]

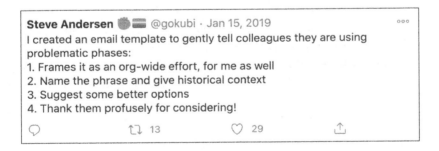

> Steve Andersen 🕊️▪️ @gokubi · Jan 15, 2019   ○○○
> I created an email template to gently tell colleagues they are using problematic phases:
> 1. Frames it as an org-wide effort, for me as well
> 2. Name the phrase and give historical context
> 3. Suggest some better options
> 4. Thank them profusely for considering!
>
> 💬   ↻ 13   ♡ 29   ⬆️

Now for an important "don't": Don't just call someone a racist or sexist or homophobe to their face. "If your goal is to communicate, loaded terms get you nowhere," says Dr. K. E. Supriya, an expert on the role of gender and cultural identity in communication. "If you simply call someone a racist, a wall goes up."[34]

When you see something, do you say something? Do you push back? Do you say, "Not cool" or ask, "What makes you say that?" If not, now's the time to start.

It can happen anywhere

No one wants to believe that their own workplace is oppressive or racist or overflowing with sexist rhetoric. In fact, "That doesn't happen here" is often the default response when leaders are informed about bias within their organization's own walls.

Yet again, defensiveness serves no purpose. Dedicated allies learn to accept that *we are all biased.* Yes, even highly rated, award-winning, utterly delightful workplaces employ people who have prejudices! Yes, even tiny, scrappy startups will have ingrained biases! Yes, it absolutely can happen on your home turf.

When Ellen Pao lost her gender discrimination suit against venture capital firm Kleiner Perkins Caufield & Byers in 2015, the *New York Times* approached me to comment. I responded:

> Many men in [Silicon] Valley genuinely believe that their company is a meritocracy. They think that the gender problem is something that happens somewhere else. It's my sincere hope that because Kleiner is so well known, they'll see that this problem is not at the corner. It's at the heartbeat. And after this, we'll have a series of cautionary tales about what not to do going forward.[35]

When leaders refuse to believe that bad behavior is happening under their own roofs, they do their organizations a disservice. Their denial prevents them from learning and growing, from addressing issues that negatively affect the women, BIPOC, and other people from marginalized groups who work so hard for the communal success of their organizations. If leaders fall into patterns of denial, their companies may garner reputations as workplaces that are unfriendly to workers from underrepresented groups, and they will have increasing difficulty with hiring a diverse workforce. It's a domino effect that leads to a nasty cascade of repercussions.

Instead, if you are in a position of privilege, resist the urge to say, "That doesn't happen here." Especially if your employees or coworkers come forward and tell you that *it does*. Instead of steadfastly and stubbornly insisting that your company is already as equitable as it can be, work hard to make it even better.

Want some quick tips on how to kick-start that process? Here are three:

1. **Listen.** Spend an entire day attempting to ask questions of your colleagues instead of making statements (as often as possible!). What did you learn? How did it feel?
2. **Believe.** The next time someone tells you a story or piece of information that makes you balk, pause. Count to five and evaluate *why* you have doubts.
3. **Learn.** If you have a close relationship with a member of an underrepresented group in your company, ask if they'd be comfortable discussing inequities in your shared workplace. If they agree, ask, "How can I change my own behaviors to be more supportive?"

Allies never stop learning

When it comes to spotting other allies, here's your biggest tip-off: They're the ones humbly and eagerly asking the tough questions. They're the ones who are quick to hold themselves accountable when they screw up. They're the ones who listen compassionately and learn constantly. Those are the people you want to seek out, the people you want to observe and emulate.

Allyship involves lots of advocacy and action, but it's all built on a foundation of listening and learning. When aspiring allies charge ahead, making changes and revising policies, it isn't long before they lose sight of the real goals. If we truly want to help shift the balance of power and fully support people from marginalized groups, it is absolutely crucial to continually solicit and incorporate *their* feedback about the issues that *they* want addressed. Skip that key step, and allyship is hollow and meaningless. Listen. Learn. Do. Repeat. Doing this will imbue your actions with meaning and value, now and into the future.

Actions for Better Allies:
Listen, Believe, Learn

Being an effective ally includes the less forceful but equally important activities of listening to alternate perspectives, accepting the information that people from underrepresented groups share, and learning from their stories and one's own mistakes.

- Be vulnerable and honest when you open discussions with colleagues who have less power and privilege than you.
- Resist the urge to get defensive.
- Review the list of red-flag phrases that was included in this chapter, and speak out when you hear them.
- Take action when you see or hear about bigotry, harassment, or discrimination. Be an upstander, not a bystander.
- Accept that yes, prejudice does exist in your own workplace.

PART TWO

SHIFTING
YOUR
BEHAVIOR

4

YOUR NETWORK

In 2012, I made a big career decision. After spending more than 25 years building software products and working for prominent tech companies, I decided to strike out on my own. I was fed up with the lack of gender diversity in the software industry, and I wanted to help keep women in tech, if that's where they wanted to be. So, I created a business to advocate for women and help them advance their careers. I became a leadership coach for women.

Starting my business was, in a word, daunting. I had never run a small business. I didn't know the first thing about marketing, attracting clients, pricing my services, or closing deals.

I turned to my network for advice. But there was a problem: I hadn't invested much time in building or nurturing it. Sure, I had my fair share of connections on LinkedIn, but many of those were distant or dormant. My network was limited and frankly a bit stale, and I knew I needed to spend time shoring it up.

I started looking for networking events to attend and uncovered lots of opportunities. Women in Tech meetups. Girl Geek dinners. Women Who Code events. The Women's CLUB of Silicon Valley. Armed with my new business cards that declared me to be an "advocate for women in tech," I started networking like a champ. Or so I thought.

I met a lot of people, but I have to admit that my network-building strategy was flawed. My goal was to meet women working in tech to build awareness of my new coaching practice and hopefully land some business. I was going for a high volume of connections, assuming that the more women I met, the more clients I could book. A few engagements did shake out of my initial efforts, but, in hindsight, I should have been more strategic about who I was adding to my network. Instead of focusing on technical women like myself, I should have been targeting engineering leaders who could bring me in to coach their employees. Frankly, I should have been networking with men in positions of power.

With my flawed strategy, I built a highly homogeneous network. It was full of mostly women, who, as it turned out, were mostly white. Just like me.

How to spot a truly effective network (hint: it's diverse)

Did you know most people have largely homogenous professional networks? As I learned from a report from the Kapor Center for Social Impact, for example, 75 percent of white people don't have any people of color in their social network.[36] And, according to the 2017 "Women in the Workplace" study by Lean In and McKinsey & Company: "Women are more than five times more likely to rely on a network that is mostly female."[37]

Homogeneous networks form because of the way we network. Herminia Ibarra, a professor of organizational behavior at the London Business School, says, "Left to our own devices ... we produce networks that are 'just like me,' convenience networks."[38]

This makes sense because common interests tend to fuel networks. Let's face it; We meet new people because of our shared hobbies or other interests. At Adobe, I joined the knitting club in our San Francisco office. Meeting over lunch on Wednesdays, we got to know each other while knitting baby blankets and hats for a local nonprofit. I loved it. But, guess how many male colleagues I met via the knitting group? Zero. Sure, there are men who enjoy knitting, but none of them joined our group.

Building a professional network across lines of difference can prove difficult, especially when it involves getting outside our comfort zone. While not impossible, it can be challenging. Outside of work, men tend to hang out with their male coworkers, perhaps grabbing a beer after work, joining a virtual poker game, playing a round of golf, or going to a ball game together. By contrast, women are more likely to spend time with nonwork friends, such as book club members, fellow volunteers for a nonprofit, members of a religious organization, or, if we have kids, other parents from playgroups and school.[39] For women who handle the lion's share of housework and childcare, networking can be extra challenging. Home responsibilities can make it tough to pull off attending evening events or out-of-town conferences.

The upshot: Men network with men, women with women. Engineers network with other engineers, and marketers with other marketers. White people network with other white people, Black people network with other Black people, and Latinx people network with other Latinx people. We want people who understand us, and instinctively know that people who are similar to us are likely to relate to our challenges and triumphs. It's human nature.

It's also counterproductive. Talking among ourselves creates an echo chamber effect and limits our access to other perspectives, experiences, and resources. Networking with people in our own fields and/or people who share our same gender identities, ethnicities, educational backgrounds, and income brackets, for example, allows us to vent and swap stories, but it doesn't encourage us to learn about wildly different experiences. And it certainly doesn't open our minds to the struggles that people with different and more marginalized experiences than us face in their lives and careers.

Ivan Misner, who developed more than three thousand networking groups in sixteen countries around the world, told *Entrepreneur*:

> Some of the strongest networking groups I've seen over the past two decades are ones that are diverse in many ways. They have a good mix of members based not only on race and gender, but also on profession, age, education and experience. The more diverse your network, the more likely you are to make overlapping linkages between clusters of people. The more linkages you can make between clusters of people, the stronger your network can be.[40]

Our personal networks benefit from diversity, too. In a *Harvard Business Review* article by Paul Gompers and Silpa Kovvali titled "The Other Diversity Dividend," I read about the importance of building diverse friend networks. It turns out that friendships across lines of ethnicity and sexual orientation reduce implicit bias. And these benefits carry over to work, where expanded networks and mindsets can improve individual and organizational performance.[41] Obvious? Maybe, but how many of us actually do this?

I'm hoping that, in the future, more people will reach beyond their comfort zones and push themselves to network with people who aren't "like" them. Doing this both expands our available opportunities and expands our minds.

Networking in the #MeToo era

> 60% of managers who are men are uncomfortable participating in a common work activity with a woman, such as mentoring, working alone, or socializing together. That's a 32% jump from a year ago [2018]. —Lean In[42]

If you read the previous section and found yourself thinking, "But, I'm a guy. How on earth do I network across gender identities in *this* climate? One wrong word, joke, or choice, and I'll get thrown into the penalty box!" You might be scared you'll get fired, be sued, or ruin your career.

This is a *somewhat* understandable reaction. Research by Lean In found that men in senior leadership roles are 3.5 times more likely to feel uncertain about scheduling a work dinner with a junior-level woman than with a junior-level man.[43] And according to the Pew Research Center, 51 percent of Americans believe the #MeToo movement has made it harder for men to know how to interact with women in the workplace.[44] This dynamic feels new to many men, and many men are unsure how to navigate it without feeling fearful and vulnerable.

Many have even adopted something called "the Billy Graham rule" or "the Mike Pence rule." This is a practice where a male leader avoids spending time alone with any woman who isn't his wife. Regardless of the motivation behind it, this rule is a real thing, and it has real consequences for women and their ability to advance under male supervisors. There are both corporations and individuals who have adopted it.[45]

I've met some of these men. A business unit leader once announced during a workshop I was facilitating, "My wife gets jealous when I have a work dinner with a female coworker," and then asked, "How should I handle that?" My snarky side wanted to scream at him to go to couples' therapy. Instead, I simply recommended, "You could always bring along another coworker. Or only meet coworkers of any gender over breakfast." I'm hoping that the discussion had an impact — if not on him, then at least on the rest of the attendees.

This "Mike Pence rule" has been growing in popularity since the #MeToo movement began. In 2019, Lean In and SurveyMonkey surveyed over five thousand employed adults about harassment. As the quote above points out, more than half of male managers said that since #MeToo, they've become uncomfortable working alone, mentoring, or socializing with a woman. Why? Because they were nervous about how it would look.[46]

I'm disturbed by this trend. No one should be excluded from out-of-the-office activities where colleagues get to know each other, share ideas, and learn from each other. In an interview in *The Atlantic*, Kim Elsesser, a professor of psychology and gender at UCLA, shared an example that caught my attention:

> A boss has season tickets to see a baseball team. He generally invites men from work to join him — not because of discrimination, but because he's worried about how the invitation would be perceived if he extended it to a woman. So he invites male coworkers to the baseball game, and they discuss work — clients and upcoming projects. The boss hears these male employees' ideas, and that gives them an advantage in the workplace. As time goes by, he gives them opportunities the women just don't get.
>
> Over time, men get to know other men much better and women get to know other women much better. Men run most of our companies, and therefore they tend to be the most valuable mentors. When a promotion or a new job opportunity comes up, the man chooses the person that he knows slightly better — the person he had that beer with. Over time, this can have major repercussions.[47]

It may feel increasingly uncomfortable and complex for male leaders to be active allies to their women colleagues and employees, but shying away from interacting with women in the workplace doesn't make it any easier. And while avoiding women altogether may make some men feel more comfortable, it also has the toxic side effect of further isolating and ostracizing women in the workplace. The #MeToo movement is not meant to drive a giant wedge between people of different genders when it comes to professional networking and mentoring, but if men take a giant step back, it will.

If you are a male leader, first of all, don't become part of this trend. As my friends David Smith and Brad Johnson emphasize in their book *Good Guys: How Men Can Be Better Allies for Women in the Workplace,* "If you are a man in any sort of leadership role, intentional interaction with women in a non-negotiable job requirement."[48] So, check yourself often. Reflect back on your week and ask yourself if you avoided being alone with a coworker because of concerns that they, or others, might think it was more than a professional interaction. If the answer is "yup" or "well, maybe," there's work to do.

Next, be open and honest about your concerns. If you want to chat with a woman colleague over coffee instead of in yet another virtual meeting but worry she might take it the wrong way, say so. Try this: "How would you feel about meeting at an outdoor cafe for this meeting? If you'd be more comfortable talking on a video call, that's completely fine, too. I just thought a change of scene might be nice." Offer choices, offer an out, and you'll show the other person that their input is welcome and they're not powerless.

Finally, become a role model for others. Men, mentor a woman. Informally or formally, it can make a difference. Respond to that next email seeking your advice. Tell the women's group at your company that you are available to be a mentor. Volunteer through a formal mentoring program.

Rachana Bhide, founder of The Corner of the Court Project, which shares stories of male allies supporting women, says she's seen mentorship have a phenomenal ripple effect.

"The women's stories from our program show mentorship has far-reaching results," Bhide explains. "Many examples of men's mentorship (for example, making an introduction, offering coaching) are at zero 'cost' to the male ally; they are simple actions which build and spark outcomes. We've featured women who have developed entire product lines, started businesses, and made career pivots from a simple action from a male mentor. The trite adage of one plus one equals three, in these cases, actually becomes one plus one equals infinity when men see mentorship as an act of collaboration with the women they support."[49]

By the way, mentoring is a two-way street. When we share our experiences and advice with others, we have the opportunity to help them grow in their careers. At the same time, we can learn from them and grow in our own careers. This may be the most compelling reason why we *shouldn't* embrace "the Mike Pence rule."

Can allies attend identity-specific networking events?

I've made the case for diversifying our networks above. But if we naturally segregate by gender or race, this can prove difficult. If a man is actively seeking to increase the number of women in his professional network, is it okay for him to attend a women's event? Similarly, is it okay for a white person to attend an event for Black or Latinx people?

To gather some perspectives beyond my own, I ran a brief Twitter poll asking for input on men attending women's events. I also asked meeting organizers about their policies and did some searching online. Not surprisingly, both pros and cons surfaced.

First, the pros. By attending a women's conference, event, or meeting, men can:

- Demonstrate support for women
- Learn from the presentations and the conversations, and better understand how to be an ally
- Build empathy for what it's like to be a member of an underrepresented group
- Diversify their networks
- Spot talent for job openings at their company

And there's an upside for women when men attend these events. Women can:

- Diversify their networks with male colleagues or industry contacts
- Cultivate sponsors for their own career growth or for diversity initiatives
- Foster stronger allies for themselves and their peers

On the flip side, some women's events sell out quickly. Why should a man take a seat that would otherwise go to a deserving woman? Furthermore, many women's events, especially smaller ones, are designed to create a safer space for women to discuss their concerns. Having men in the room might constrain the dialogue, especially if those concerns are *about* men. These same concerns surface for events tailored to other underrepresented groups. Why should a white person get to show up in a space created for Black people to discuss the issues that affect them? If a cisgender individual attends an event for transgender people, the rest of the attendees may feel uncomfortable being totally candid.

Some women responded to my Twitter poll by pointing out a few issues specific to men infiltrating women's events. In short, they may be seen as having questionable motives. A sampling of quotes includes: "Guys at professional events are always hitting on me"; "They just want to check a box on their personal diversity scorecard"; and "They're annoying: desperate to find candidates to increase their company's diversity ratio."

Clearly this is not a cut-and-dried issue, and it becomes even murkier when we're talking about networking events and conferences that focus on Black or LGBTQ professionals. But I believe that allies have a lot to gain from attending certain kinds of events for underrepresented groups (the ones with open discussions versus those designed to create safe spaces for discussion) and that such groups benefit when allies participate. I also believe that there are three boxes that should be checked if you're a person with substantial privilege and you'd like to attend a gathering that's been specifically organized for people who are marginalized in a way that you are not. Make sure:

- You'll be welcome (Not sure? Check the website, or ask the organizer and respect their response.)
- You're clear on your intentions (My suggestion? To become a better ally.)
- You're prepared to listen and learn

Simple as that.

And here's a story from my own experience that highlights how easy it is to join networking events when they're held virtually (for COVID-19 safety or other reasons).

On June 19, 2020, I dialed into the keynote for the Juneteenth Conference, an event made for and featuring Black people in technology. It started with 8+ minutes of silence in honor of George Floyd, followed by an outstanding talk by Danny Thompson about his professional journey, inspired by a rapper who wanted to learn to code. Thompson spoke about going from frying chicken to helping 44 people land their first jobs in tech. His focus on helping bring positive change to his city (and his personal life) was inspiring, and left me wanting to do more to help my community. In fact, hearing his keynote made me say yes to a meeting invitation I received just days later to consider serving on a board of directors of DigitalNEST, a nonprofit focused on teaching digital skills to young adults in rural, agricultural-based cities in California. If I hadn't attended Thompson's talk, I might've passed on that meeting. Attending as an ally shaped my choices, for the better.

How to diversify your network: Getting started

"Just like me" networks can have a negative impact on creating diverse, inclusive workplaces. Those who are involved in hiring new staff naturally look to the people who are part of their professional networks, because they know and trust them, but when those networks are homogenous, this translates to favoring and advocating for folks like themselves. Depending on referrals is standard, and if those referrals come from a homogeneous network, it results in just hiring more homogeneity. It's also common for leaders to favor their network members when assigning career-advancing stretch goals, reviewing candidates for promotions and key spots during reorganizations, and creating succession plans. We instinctively bolster the people we know and trust, who are almost always, without fail, people just like us.

As of the writing of this book, white men still hold the majority of senior-level positions in U.S. companies across all sorts of industries. And because white men generally have networks brimming with other white men, this means women, BIPOC, and members of other underrepresented groups are less likely to have access to the people who can help them boost their careers.[50]

In other words, if you only open doors to people in your network, chances are they'll be for people who are similar to you. If you've read this far, you'll undoubtedly recognize that to be problematic (or so I hope!). Luckily, diversifying your network isn't the onerous task you may fear it to be. There are many simple, easy actions that can be taken to widen your professional circle outside your comfort zone.

The next time you're grabbing coffee at the office, or attending an event or conference, in person or virtually:

- Reach out to people who don't look like you. Introduce yourself to someone of a different gender, race, age, or other visible difference. Get to know them and stay in touch with them. Perhaps you'll be able to learn from them or introduce them to a career opportunity down the road.

- Attend industry events for people who are different from you. Each is an opportunity to listen and learn about their experiences, and of course, to expand your network. Not sure if you'd be welcome? Check the event information or ask the organizer. Many such groups and gatherings are open to allies.

- Volunteer for an organization that serves a diverse populace or operates outside your immediate neighborhood.

- Try a conference on a topic that isn't your exact area of expertise. Attend any panels that feature a diversity of speakers, and follow them afterward on social media. Take the time to connect with other attendees.

- At every company event, networking opportunity, and industry party, force yourself to talk to one total stranger who is different from you. Just walk up, introduce yourself, and ask them what they're working on right now that excites them.

Of course, there are also many ways to expand and diversify your connections online. Consider:

- Joining Slack channels or other discussion forums for underrepresented groups (after asking first if you'd be welcome)
- Listening to a variety of podcasts by or featuring people from marginalized communities
- Following people of different genders, ethnic backgrounds, sexual orientations and identities, ages, abilities, and so forth on social media

If you're ready to make an even bigger move outside your comfort zone, offer to mentor someone who is a member of a marginalized group. This will give you the opportunity to both learn *and* teach, as well as grow *and* foster the growth of another. (More on this in Chapter 12.)

Actions for Better Allies:
Diversify Your Network

Most of us have largely homogeneous networks. Here are some tips for ensuring that your network is diverse and more effective:

- Do a network inventory. List out the people you feel to be your top ten contacts. Are any of them marginalized in ways that you are not? If not, start in your own backyard: Who within your own organization could be a great addition to your current network?
- Attend an event where diversity will be the topic of discussion. Listen and learn.
- The next time you attend an event of *any* kind, introduce yourself to someone who doesn't look like you.
- If you are interested in attending an event that caters specifically to a group of which you are not a member, ask the organizers before showing up.
- Seek out media, including podcasts and blogs, by people who are different from you.

5

ORGANIZING AND ATTENDING EVENTS

Imagine attending a party at a conference. You've had a long day of participating in group sessions, networking with colleagues, and absorbing tons of information. You're just scoping out the room to see if anyone you know has already arrived when some stranger hands you their empty plate to be cleared. Or asks you to get them another drink. If you're Black or Brown, you might not have to use your imagination, because you might very well have had this experience yourself. I've heard from engineers of color that they've been mistaken for members of the catering staff at events they attend. One turban-clad software engineer told me it happened to him at a reception, even though he was wearing a tuxedo — another guest approached him and asked him to refill one of the buffet items. And get this. At a party in 2003, another guest asked then state senator Barack Obama to fetch him a drink.[51]

Now imagine meeting someone at an event and the first words out of their mouth are, "Do you work in HR?" If you're a woman, you've most likely lost count of the number of times this has happened to you. I've experienced this one firsthand: Not too long ago, I visited my partner Tim at his new office in San Francisco. As he gave me a tour, he introduced me to some of his colleagues. It was great to put some faces to the names I'd been hearing over dinner since he started a few months earlier. What wasn't so great was meeting one man in particular, who said, "I hear you used to work at Adobe. So, did you work in HR or marketing?"

I felt like growling at him, but instead, I bit my lip and replied, "Actually, I was a vice president of engineering."

Perhaps people in your very own office assume that you're not in a technical role. As one woman shared via Twitter, "The chief technology officer said to me, 'What do you do here? Business analyst?' I was a developer with an award on the wall behind him."

Now, there's absolutely nothing wrong with working in HR or being a business analyst or holding any other non-technical role. It's the implication that women *never* work in technical roles that really burns.

Here's another scenario: You've pulled your wheelchair up to a table and are sipping a cocktail at the post-conference party while chatting with a guy from another company. He asks how you ended up attending, then looks astounded when you say, "I'm one of the speakers."

I hear these stories all too often from members of marginalized groups — stories where people with deep expertise are presumed not to have any. Where others make the wrong assumptions about them, over and over again. Where people from underrepresented groups get subtle (and overt) messages that they don't belong.

It's a thing, and it adds up. It's like death by a thousand cuts. Only it's a thousand microaggressions doing the damage.

Understanding and combating microaggressions

Never heard the term "microaggression" before? You're not alone. What the term describes has existed for hundreds of years, but it has only carried this particular label since the 1970s. Columbia University psychology professor Derald Wing Sue, PhD, defines the term as follows:

> Microaggressions are the everyday verbal, nonverbal, and environmental slights, snubs, or insults, whether intentional or unintentional, which communicate hostile, derogatory, or negative messages to target persons based solely upon their marginalized group membership. In many cases, these hidden messages may invalidate the group identity or experiential reality of target persons, demean them on a personal or group level, communicate they are lesser human beings, suggest they do not belong with the majority group, threaten and intimidate, or relegate them to inferior status and treatment.[52]

Sounds pretty awful, right? Anyone who's been on the receiving end can confirm that *it is*. In fact, for some people, microaggressions are harder to bear than more overt bigotry because they're subtle but ever-present, small but ongoing. They wear a person down slowly over time, like dripping water on a stone, gradually convincing them that they're less-than, through barely noticeable social cues and offhand remarks.

Here are some examples of microaggressions that frequently surface in workplaces:

- **You've got the wrong room. This is the engineers/managers meeting.** Just like at the hypothetical party above, it's fairly common for people to assume that people from underrepresented groups couldn't possibly hold technical or leadership roles.
- **Where are you *really* from?** When BIPOC are asked this, it implies that they can't possibly be a "real"

American. Or worse, that they don't "belong" in this country.

- **Oops! Wrong person.** When there are only two Black people, women, queer people, Muslims, or members of another underrepresented group at a meeting, event, or company, odds are good that someone will get them mixed up, sending the message that they "all look the same" and aren't seen as individuals.
- **Your English is so good/you're so articulate.** Why are you surprised? Because the person has a non-Anglo name? Because of their skin color?
- **You look so young!** This implies that you're surprised the person in question is experienced or seasoned, which undermines their authority. In addition, if the recipient is a woman, it puts focus squarely on her appearance instead of her accomplishments.[53]

Many of these may seem harmless; some even masquerade as compliments. Many of them are handed out by well-meaning people who have no idea that they're being condescending or marginalizing. But effective allies must learn to be aware of microaggressions like these so they can avoid them at all costs.

When a person from an underrepresented group has their credentials called into question, it amounts to an "unconscious demotion." Dr. Suzanne Wertheim coined this term to describe the unthinking habit of assuming that someone holds a position lower in status or expertise than they actually do.[54] In 2018, the *New York Times* interviewed about a dozen professionals of color who shared their experiences with unconscious demotions. Like how others assumed that they were part of the help. Or that they weren't qualified to treat patients. Or that they should be patted down when entering a courthouse (when white colleagues weren't).[55] Wertheim points out that this pattern of thoughtless microaggressions isn't just aggravating, it's truly harmful.

> While mistaking a doctor for a nurse or a sysadmin for a personal assistant might feel like just a small mistake, the negative effects on the person being unconsciously demoted can be real and long lasting.[56]

So how can we do better? How can we bypass microaggressions and avoid handing out unconscious demotions? Here are some strategies:

- **Accept that microaggressions are real.** If you haven't been on the receiving end of this behavior, you may feel like the people describing it are "exaggerating" its effects. They're not. Denying the existence and power of microaggressions is counterproductive. Believe people when they say they're being adversely affected.
- **Create a forum for discussion.** The best way to root out an insidious problem is to shine a bright light on it. Consider hosting events or discussion groups to highlight microaggressions, teach people how to spot them, and train them to avoid the associated behaviors.[57]
- **Stand up against microaggressions.** Once you know how to spot one, speak up when you witness one. (More on this later in this chapter.)

Professional events are rife with microaggressions against underrepresented groups, and plenty of them foster more overtly harmful behaviors, too. Everyone from organizers to attendees can end up making people from marginalized groups feel unwelcome, targeted, unseen, or even objectified. Want to avoid hosting (or attending) conferences and gatherings that allow prejudiced activities and language? Then read on!

How to make professional events more inclusive

Whether you're booking speakers, choosing menus, delivering a keynote, or simply attending as a participant, you can help make conferences, meetings, and other gatherings more welcoming to all attendees.

Utilize a diverse planning committee

Creating a diverse planning committee is one of the best ways to create an inclusive event. An organizing body that has a variety of life experiences and perspectives can make sure that others from their own underrepresented group feel comfortable and/or included at the event. Make sure that the planning and leadership of the event includes women, BIPOC, LGBTQ people, people with disabilities, and others from underrepresented groups.

Make sure that events feature diverse voices

In early 2018, the RSA security conference announced their 2018 speaker lineup: Nineteen keynotes by men, and only one by a woman. To make matters worse, the woman keynote speaker was Monica Lewinsky, who would speak not about technology but about "The Price of Shame." Out of frustration with the lineup, the OURSA conference was born. (Notice the clever play on words? Organizers reclaimed the topic by naming their gathering "our" SA.)

At OURSA, every single speaker was from a background that is typically underrepresented in the privacy and security field — and it was organized in record time. Clearly these voices were out there, ready, willing, and more than able to share their technical expertise. A diverse organizing committee invited and attracted a diverse set of speakers. Those speakers, in turn, attracted a diverse group of attendees. And that led to an inclusive event.

If you're organizing an event and are having trouble identifying speakers from underrepresented groups, here are two suggestions: Diversify your network (following some of the tips in Chapter 4), and ask *every white male speaker* to recommend at least one person from an underrepresented group to deliver a talk.

If you're considering attending an event but see a lineup of speakers that's overwhelmingly homogeneous, contact the organizers and ask about it. Suggest people from your own network who could be swapped in or contacted for future speaking opportunities (after asking them first if they'd like to be recommended).

Create a code of conduct

Everyone deserves to feel comfortable and safe within a community. A code of conduct is one indicator that the organizers of a conference or other event want to provide a harassment-free experience for everyone.

Before accepting a speaking engagement or registering for an event, ask if there's a code of conduct. Of course, it's not enough for there to just be a code of conduct. It also needs to be enforced. Ask about that, too. (More on this later in this chapter.)

Make sure that events are fully accessible

If an event is being held in the United States, it's likely that the rented space already complies with the Americans with Disabilities Act (ADA), but there's so much more that's needed in order to make an event truly inclusive. Many disabilities are invisible and others are not related to physical needs, but all merit respect and accommodation. Are ramps clearly marked? Are pathways wide enough that people with wheelchairs and scooters can navigate them? Is type large and high-contrast? Will simultaneous sign language translation and closed captions be offered? The ADA offers a comprehensive document titled "A Planning Guide for Making Temporary Events Accessible to People with Disabilities" online.[58] It's definitely worth a look.

Planning an event and not sure what accommodations you should provide? On your event registration form, provide a point of contact and invite attendees to let you know their needs in advance — and be prepared to respond to and meet whatever needs the attendees specify.

Feature a diversity of people in slides and media

We send subtle messages whenever and wherever we use images. In presentations and pitch decks. In user personas. In marketing collateral. In blog posts. On websites. If these materials show only white people, or men, or people with no visible disabilities, for example, it reinforces stereotypes.

It may be understated, but the simple act of using stock photos that feature BIPOC and other underrepresented groups makes a difference. Seeing someone who looks like you in the promotions for a conference or event is a clear signal that people who look like you will be welcome. Representation matters. Need some sources? Check out the "Additional Resources" section at the end of this book for a list of stock photography sites featuring people from underrepresented groups.

Provide financial assistance

To encourage and support a diverse group of attendees, consider providing scholarships, travel stipends, or lower registration rates to people from underrepresented groups. Think about offering child care services at no charge, like the Grace Hopper Celebration of Women in Computing started doing a few years ago.

Offer mocktails with those cocktails

Imagine an event where the only available food is pepperoni pizza. Imagine this is the case because pepperoni pizza is traditionally served at all industry parties. Now imagine being lactose intolerant, someone who keeps kosher, a vegetarian or vegan, or someone with celiac disease. If you knew that you'd have no other choices besides pepperoni pizza, would you ever attend events? If you did, would you feel welcome? What if you just didn't like pepperoni pizza? Think you might get tired of explaining that every time a colleague offered you a slice?

This is a bit of an extreme example, but goes a long way toward highlighting the plight of the nondrinker. There are myriad reasons someone might choose not to drink alcohol, including religious, age-related, pregnancy, addiction, and medical reasons. Additionally, some people might not want to get buzzed or just don't like alcohol! Absolutely none of these reasons are anyone's business, and absolutely none of them are legitimate excuses for making an event attendee feel ostracized or left out.

If there's a budget for fancy cocktails and craft beers, there's a budget for mocktails, kombucha, bubble tea, and so forth. Planning an inclusive event when it comes to beverages means providing an equal number and quality of alcoholic and nonalcoholic drink options. That's right, canned soda and orange juice from concentrate won't cut it. The point is to make nondrinkers feel like valued equals, not second-class citizens.[59]

Review the speakers' slides

If you're an event organizer and have the opportunity to review slides before your event, look out for risqué, insensitive, or offensive content.

During the summer of 2018, while giving an acceptance speech for a distinguished award, a researcher showed several pictures of "scantily clad female students" doing field research. As the Rochester *Democrat and Chronicle* reported, "The photographs were risqué enough that conference organizers added blue boxes to cover parts of the women's bodies."[60]

Better would have been to reject the slides completely.

Look holistically at the experience

Yup, it's 2021, and I'm here stating what should be obvious. Sexualized, pinup images don't belong on swag or any professional material. It's offensive and derogatory toward women. And yet at a recent InfoSec World conference, Security Weekly handed out a bumper sticker that said "code naked" with a pinup silhouette (there were T-shirts, too).

As someone said in an online discussion about the sticker, "I might have thought those were awesome … when I was 14." Spot on.

As an organizer, think holistically about the experience people will have at your event: the conference theme, talk titles, and even playlists used between speakers or leading up to a plenary address. I heard from someone who attended the LGBTQ Task Force's national Creating Change conference, and right before a panel discussion on HIV/AIDS, the dance song "Die Young" by Kesha was played. It was horrifically insensitive.

When I spoke at the Linux Foundations' Open Source Summit in San Diego in 2019, I witnessed firsthand their focus on running a conference that's inclusive. Here's what they offered:

- A code of conduct (and event staff who had been trained in incident response)
- No all-male panels
- A diverse group of keynote speakers
- A nursing room
- Complimentary childcare
- Venue accessibility
- A quiet room (for attendees who, for any reason, can't interact with others at that time)
- All-gender restrooms

- Communication stickers (indicating if attendees are open to communication, only if they know you, or none at all)
- Pronoun stickers

Gather feedback

After an event, many organizers send out brief surveys to get feedback and look for ways to improve it the next time. Why not also ask if the event could have been more inclusive, and if so, how?

When you see something, say something

Professional events are where people from across an industry gather to meet, exchange ideas, and network. When conferences and events feel unwelcoming or hostile to members of marginalized groups, they are less likely to engage or attend. This translates to excluding them from some of the most important connection opportunities in the field, preventing them from forging valuable relationships and advancing their careers. And this, in turn, means that people who choose to say nothing after witnessing microaggressions, offensive jokes, or other inappropriate behavior at events are enabling this phenomenon. We become complicit. There is no neutral. It's our duty as allies to speak up.

Of course, "speaking up" is never easy. Western society trains us to avoid confrontation and conflict, so marching up to someone who just dropped a racist remark and saying, "That's not okay" can feel deeply uncomfortable. Before digging into actionable strategies, here's a quick reminder about in-person callouts: They involve words. Just words. Telling someone they're acting like a jerk at a conference doesn't hold the same risks as relaying that same message to a drunk person at a bar. You are unlikely to come to blows. In fact, it's probable that the worst that'll happen is some social awkwardness and tense silence. You can survive this. You can do this. The mere fact that most people aren't brave enough to confront bigoted behavior means that *when you do*, it is likely to have a huge impact.

So how do you go about it? The easiest way is simply to have some scripted responses in your back pocket. In the moment, you might freeze up and doubt yourself, so memorizing a few stock callouts is a great way to prepare yourself to confront inappropriate behavior.

Responses to witnessing microaggressions

- **"What makes you say/think that?"** See someone telling a Latina that her "English is fantastic"? Ask them why they're mentioning it. Force them to examine their motives and mental connections.
- **"I'd like to hear the rest of what ___ was saying."** This is a useful response to interruptions.
- **"That made me feel uncomfortable."**

Responses to offensive jokes

- **"I don't get it. Can you explain the joke to me?"** Again, this forces the speaker to dig into their reasoning aloud, which brings bigotry to light.
- **"That wasn't funny."**
- **"That's against our code of conduct."** Naturally, only use this one in cases where there is an actual code in place.
- **"Wow, that was awkward."**
- **"Did you really just say that?"**
- **"Actually, that's a really bad stereotype."**

Responses to social or physical harassment

- **"Everything okay here?"** Just checking in verbally with someone who looks uncomfortable can be the equivalent of throwing them a lifeline.
- **"Not cool."** Notice someone flirting or getting physically close to a woman (and sensing that it's unwanted)? Call it out with these simple words.
- **"We don't do that here."** A useful phrase for enforcing cultural norms that are inclusive.

As I mentioned briefly toward the end of Chapter 3, direct verbal accusations of racism, sexism, or bigotry of any kind are often met with hostility. Yet another reason why these formulas are so helpful: They target the action, not the person. They curb the behavior quickly and directly, without allowing the offender to shift into angry defensiveness. You won't be able to turn a racist into an anti-racist just by saying they are racist, but you will be able to interrupt a microaggression or act of harassment before it plays out.

When witnessing offensive, harmful, or harassing behavior of any kind, each of us has a simple choice: Call it out or be complicit. It's important to note that this applies even if no one present is personally offended or targeted by it.

How to craft a useful code of conduct

Because most of the problematic behaviors at events aren't illegal, and because many are subtle and social in nature, it can be helpful to write, publish, and enforce rules specific to an event. When it comes to curbing microaggressions and harassment, a code of conduct can make a huge difference.

The purpose of a code of conduct is to protect members of a community from harm by other members of the community, even if that harm is unintended. In fact, thoughtful and impactful codes of conduct address behaviors that the general population may view as socially acceptable but that are unacceptable within a particular community, group, or professional context.

Here's an example from tech company Mapbox:

Events Code of Conduct

All attendees, speakers, sponsors, vendors, partners and volunteers at our conferences/events are required to adhere to the following Code of Conduct. Mapbox event organizers will enforce this Code throughout the event.

Our aim in hosting events is to build community. To that end, our goal is to create an environment where everyone feels welcome to participate, speak up, ask questions, and engage in conversation. We invite all those who participate in this event to help us create safe and positive experiences for everyone.

Every Mapbox event/conference is dedicated to providing a harassment-free environment for everyone, regardless of gender, gender identity and expression, age, sexual orientation, disability, physical appearance, body size, race, ethnicity, or religion (or lack thereof). We do not tolerate harassment of participants in any form. Sexual language and imagery is not appropriate during any aspect of the event/conference, including talks, workshops, parties, social media such as Twitter, or other online media.

Expected Behavior

Participate in an authentic and active way. In doing so, you contribute to the health and longevity of the community.

Exercise consideration and respect in your speech and actions.

Attempt collaboration before conflict.

Refrain from demeaning, discriminatory, or harassing behavior and speech.

Be mindful of your surroundings and of your fellow participants. Alert community leaders if you notice a dangerous situation, someone in distress, or violations of this Code of Conduct, even if they seem inconsequential.

Conference participants violating these rules may be sanctioned or expelled from the event/conference without a refund at the discretion of the organizers. Participants asked to stop any harassing behavior are expected to comply immediately.

Reporting an Incident

If you see, overhear or experience a violation of the Code of Conduct during an event, please seek out the nearest Mapbox team member to escalate your complaint. If you cannot find a team member, or would like to report a violation after an event, you may email events@mapbox.com.[61]

Note the essential components:

- A statement that the event organizers will not tolerate certain behaviors
- A description of the inappropriate behaviors and who they might target
- An explanation of the possible actions or sanctions that will be taken against offenders
- Directions on what to do if one experiences or sees unacceptable behavior
- A list of the ways the organizers will support anyone who has been targeted
- Indication that anyone unwilling to comply should not attend

Codes of conduct can be considerably more detailed if there is a need, which may be the case for events with a history of some specific kind of inappropriate behavior. However, all that's really needed are these six elements to create a clear, enforceable code of conduct.

Valerie Aurora, principal consultant at Frame Shift Consulting, points out that there are several elements that should be *omitted* from codes of conduct. Don't call out behaviors that aren't common in a community (e.g., juggling in the aisles during events), and don't call out crimes or behaviors that are universally unacceptable (e.g., stealing money). Doing this distracts from what's essential about the code and insults your attendees. Don't mandate politeness or other forms of "proper" behavior, as these are deeply subjective, difficult to enforce, and often serve to further marginalize underrepresented groups. Finally, don't list rules that won't or can't be enforced. Codes of conduct must be backed up with action.[62]

A code of conduct needs to prove that actions have consequences. It will only be an effective tool for protecting conference attendees and participants if everyone knows for sure that it will be enforced.

Allies can help enforce codes of conduct. Allies can and should work harder to ensure that the events they sponsor and attend feel safe for all, including people from underrepresented groups. Right now, discussions of tech events are brimming with appalling stories about harassment, sexism, racism, and microaggressions. Beyond tech, the news is full of stories about members of marginalized groups feeling threatened, demeaned, disrespected, or worse in their places of work. Together, we can force those numbers downward until professional gatherings become the welcoming, equitable, uplifting events they ought to be.

Actions for Better Allies:
Make Events Welcoming

Too many professional events can be inhospitable for members of underrepresented groups. Here are some ways to help turn the tide:

- Make events inclusive. Feature diverse voices, offer interesting nonalcoholic drinks, create and enforce a code of conduct, practice full accessibility, provide financial assistance, and push back on risqué images and offensive swag.
- Before attending or agreeing to speak at an event, make sure there will be a code of conduct as well as other support for attendees from underrepresented groups.
- If you see a lineup of speakers that's homogeneous, contact the organizers and demand better.
- Look out for microaggressions (or worse) during an event, and take action when you spot them.

6

MEETINGS IN THE WORKPLACE

Talk to a woman who works in an office, and she'll tell you about a time (or two or ten) when she felt frustrated, if not downright dejected, in a meeting. Perhaps she was asked to take notes or get coffee, even though those aren't her responsibilities. Perhaps she was talked over or ignored. Perhaps someone claimed credit for the idea she had proposed earlier. If she's a woman of color, she's likely experienced all of the above in various infuriating combinations. Even in companies where codified policies are intentionally equitable, meeting culture can be almost comically biased.

I've seen this in action myself. Not too long ago, I sat on a fundraising committee for my alma mater. Our goal was to endow the computer science department's undergraduate teaching assistant program. During one of our calls, I suggested we approach a certain alum, a prominent venture capitalist. While he hadn't studied computer science, his investments could benefit from a larger pool of software engineers graduating from our university. I thought we might convince him to support our fundraising by pointing out how it would pay off for him down the road.

I raised this idea on the call, but it didn't go anywhere. Perhaps we had other contacts that seemed more promising at the time. Perhaps I wasn't convincing enough. Either way, we didn't pursue my suggestion.

Imagine my surprise when I received an email a few weeks later from a member of our committee asking me what I thought of approaching that same alum. After picking up my jaw from the floor, I quickly wrote back, "I think it's a great idea. That's why I suggested it in our last meeting."

To his credit, he replied, "I remembered that right after I sent the message. Sorry." If only every person in a leadership position were this self-aware.

Over the years, I've trained myself to call it out when a guy co-opts one of my ideas. However, other women and members of other marginalized groups may not feel comfortable being so bold or may fear censure if they speak up for themselves. This, among other reasons, is why allies can and should be doing this.

Here's how to spot situations where you can take action, along with suggested actions to make meetings more balanced and equitable.

"Manterruptions"

A study by researchers at Northwestern University analyzed hearings of the U.S. Supreme Court over the past twelve years. The study found that women justices were interrupted three times more often than men, and that women initiated only four percent of the interruptions overall.[63] The study was revisited in late 2019, and its authors reported, "Our results show that women are interrupted more than men, which compromises their ability to achieve their goals during oral arguments."[64]

Then there's the historic 2020 vice presidential debate when Mike Pence tried to cut off Kamala Harris mid-sentence. She calmly replied, "Mr. Vice President, I'm speaking." When he laughed at her statement, she simply repeated, "I'm speaking."[65]

Guess what? The same pattern appears across the tech industry and in the vast majority of corporate cultures. "Manterruptions" are a thing, and they're probably happening within your team.

There are a host of reasons why guys may be more comfortable or skilled at interrupting others. It may be that it's culturally acceptable. Or that cisgender men's vocal cords are longer, resulting in deeper voices that project well and help them break into conversations. Or it could be that women have been socialized to say, "Excuse me ..." or "May I ask ..." when beginning a thought, making it easier to be interrupted.

According to Deborah Tannen, a professor of linguistics at Georgetown University, women may also be easy targets for interruption because they are already fearful of appearing too talkative. In an article for *Time*, she wrote:

> One reason women tend to speak less at meetings, in my view, is that they don't want to come across as talking too much. It's a verbal analogue to taking up physical space. ... When they talk in a formal setting, many women try to take up less verbal space by being more succinct, speaking in a lower voice and speaking in a more tentative way. Women have good reason for such caution — what I've described as the double bind. If they talk in ways associated with authority, they can be seen as too aggressive, and subject to the damning labels so readily applied to them. But if they don't — if they hold back in these and other ways — they risk being underestimated.[66]

Tannen also pointed out that even when women are specifically asked to weigh in, they might get interrupted. For instance, at the 2017 World Science Festival, a lone woman panelist was ignored for a full hour before the male moderator asked for her input. When she started to speak, he almost immediately began speaking himself, giving his own interpretations of her theories.[67] Here's a more recent example. In November 2020, a reporter asked a member of Australia's Parliament, Anne Ruston, about the government's culture for women. Just as she started to answer, Prime Minister Scott Morrison cut her off and made it all about himself, emphasizing how seriously he treats the issue of sexual misconduct.[68]

Regardless of the reasons — and regardless of the gender identity of the person being interrupted — allies have a role to play in creating inclusive meetings. When you work to minimize interruptions, you create a more equitable workplace, with the added bonus of helping everyone know that they're valued members of the team. Here are some everyday actions to take in your next meeting to help ensure that all voices are heard:

- When someone is interrupted, interject and say you'd like to hear them finish.
- If you see someone struggling to break into the conversation, say you'd like to hear other points of view.
- If you see a "repeat offender" who interrupts frequently, pull them aside and point it out.
- Maintain eye contact and stay focused on the person who was interrupted. Not only does it demonstrate your support for that person, but your body language also helps direct the conversation back to them. (Thanks to Evin Robinson for this suggestion.[69])
- Nominate a "gatekeeper" to keep the conversations on track, perhaps using the "meeting role cards" from Frame Shift Consulting.[70]

"Bro-propriation" and idea hijacking

Let's say a person of color says something insightful or even game-changing in a meeting, only to have it dismissed or ignored. Then someone else says the same thing later and it's well-received — or maybe even heralded. While the second person (often a white man) gets the kudos, the person who originally said it starts fuming inside.

This scenario is all too common, and the frustration is understandable. Allies can borrow a page from a group of women who figured out how to stop "bro-propriation" in its tracks.

In staff meetings during Barack Obama's first term as president, women adopted a strategy they called "amplification." When one of the women staffers made a key point, other women would repeat it and give credit to its author. This approach forced others in the room to recognize the contribution — and denied them the ability to claim it as their own.[71]

Women aren't the only ones who can amplify the voices of other women, and Black people aren't the only ones who can amplify the voices of other Black people. Anyone can do it for someone who is less likely to be heard. I try to do it myself in meetings I attend. Of course, there are times when I'm not quite on the ball, and I miss the opportunity to amplify an idea contributed by someone from an underrepresented group. If someone else repeats it later in the meeting, I remind everyone who originated it, saying something like, "Great idea. Thanks to Lydia for surfacing it earlier."

And that's not all. I strive to give people credit for saying the same brilliant idea, even if they did so in a previous meeting. Here's what that might look like: "I like that idea a lot. In fact, when Ana brought that up last week in our one-on-one, I learned the following ..."

Not only do I want to amplify Ana's idea, I also hope to show her respect and help her build credibility by saying that I learned from her.

Another way to combat idea hijacking? Give credit to the project owner, even if they aren't in the room. Here's a good reminder of the simple yet important action of acknowledging someone's work, even (or especially) if they aren't present. Molly Peeples, an astronomer, tweeted: [72]

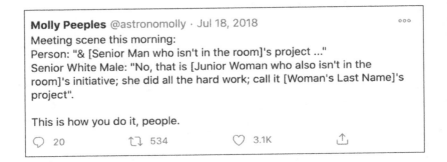

Molly Peeples @astronomolly · Jul 18, 2018   ooo
Meeting scene this morning:
Person: "& [Senior Man who isn't in the room]'s project ..."
Senior White Male: "No, that is [Junior Woman who also isn't in the room]'s initiative; she did all the hard work; call it [Woman's Last Name]'s project".

This is how you do it, people.

   ○ 20   ↻ 534   ♡ 3.1K   ↑

Allies can use their positions of privilege to stop idea hijacking in its tracks. Let's amplify and showcase the ideas coming from the marginalized people all around us. Let's make this happen.

Off-topic questions and showboating

When Representative Alexandria Ocasio-Cortez was first running for office, conservative commentator Ben Shapiro challenged her to a debate, offering to donate $10,000 to her campaign or a charity of choice if she accepted. [73] Shapiro was not running for office at all — much less as an opponent to Ocasio-Cortez — and his offer of payment would likely have been a campaign violation. This was not an offer made in good faith, this was showboating. After attempting to ignore the gambit for a day or so, Ocasio-Cortez responded via Twitter, saying: "Just like catcalling, I don't owe a response to unsolicited requests from men with bad intentions. And also like catcalling, for some reason they feel entitled to one."[74]

In presentations during meetings, a similar phenomenon can happen. People might ask off-topic questions to test presenters, undermine their credibility, and make themselves look smart in the process. It's a power play that's been used for years and can be incredibly distracting, forcing someone who was in a position of authority at the beginning of the meeting to suddenly have to defend their expertise.

As Ocasio-Cortez pointed out, women don't owe a response to off-topic requests from men (or anyone else). Marginalized people shouldn't have to defend themselves when disruptors feel the need to question their credentials. Allies can be on the lookout for these kinds of questions and shut them down.

Want an example of how an ally handled showboating beautifully? Hilary J. Scarsella — an expert in trauma, theology, and religious practice — told her Facebook audience about an experience she had at an airport after speaking at a conference. In a nutshell, she was sitting next to another speaker from the conference, and a man sitting across from them started a conversation. When he heard about the conference they'd spoken at, he launched into a diatribe about her area of expertise.

And then an epic and inspiring thing happened. As the man stood up to catch his plane, the other speaker leaned over and said, "Dude, you missed an opportunity. You had an expert in theology and trauma sitting in front of you. You say you're interested in these things but you didn't ask her a single question. You didn't try to learn anything at all from her." The speaker continued: "You know she has advanced degrees and is published but you just tried to show her that you know more about her work than she does. You missed out. Big fail, man."[75]

Well played.

Meeting housework

Meetings generate office housework. From taking minutes to scheduling follow-ups to clearing coffee cups from the table before leaving the room, there are always a bunch of administrative tasks that need to get done. Women tend to absorb these tasks, either because they're asked to or because they simply roll up their sleeves and get the job done.

You can avoid this pattern by making office housework tasks rotating responsibilities for your regular meetings. Set up a schedule for taking minutes, clearing the table, and so forth. For one-off meetings, consider asking only white men to do these tasks, in order to send a strong disrupt-the-status-quo message: "Hey Mark — could you bring the leftover pizza over to the kitchen on your way out? And stick a note on them that they're up for grabs."

(Much, much more on this in Chapter 7.)

Misdirected questions

A few years back, Geraldine Mongold was working as an IT project manager at a construction company. In meetings, she was usually the only woman in the room, and the guys around the table would direct their questions to Andy, her key stakeholder. Recognizing this pattern, Andy always stepped back and said, "Geraldine is the project manager, I'm just the procurement guy."

In a similar vein, information security leader Chad Loder recalls attending customer meetings with one of his employees, Susan, a sales engineer who could answer detailed technical questions about their company's product. All too often, customers would direct all of their questions to him, not Susan. He would say, "Well, Susan wrote the API for this," and turn the conversation over to her.

Geraldine and Susan are not alone. In the 2016 "Elephant in the Valley" survey, more than two hundred women working in tech positions were polled.[76] Of women with at least ten years of experience working in tech, 84 percent said they had seen a question directed toward a male colleague when they themselves were the most qualified person in the meeting to answer it. And it's not just men who are guilty of this, because people of all gender identities are taught to assume that men naturally hold more power.

This trend also isn't limited to tech. I heard the following from Elizabeth Giorgi, founder and CEO of video production companies Soona and Mighteor:

> Over the years, one of the most common things that happens is when we are meeting with a new client, they will often assume one of my male colleagues is the founder. I have been so fortunate that the men of character I work with have often quickly clarified. However, I am also fervent in clearing it up myself. There are many subtle ways to do this. My favorite is to wait until the conversation starts to flow and saying something simple like, "When I founded this company …" or "As the owner of this organization …" These statements show confidence, they clarify the question at hand, and they provide an opportunity to educate without shaming.[77]

Chances are good that misdirected questions surface in meetings at your company, too. As an ally, redirect the question to the most qualified person. All it takes is a simple "Deepa is the expert on that topic. Let's hear from her" or "Elizabeth is our founder. She's the best person to answer your question."

Economy seating

If you observe coworkers in meetings, you'll likely notice white men sitting in the center seats around the table. Members of underrepresented groups, by contrast, often gravitate toward the ends of the table and the edges of the room, away from positions that convey status. In other words, they take seats in the economy section.

Allies can invite marginalized people to take the power seats. In fact, allies can go even further and offer to swap seats with them. Here's how: "Sarah, I know you're going to make some killer points today. Why don't you take my seat so everyone can hear you better." Or, make some room at the table and say, "Omar, would you sit by me today? This is really the best seat in the house."

Enlisting a buddy

Many meetings have back-channels, with key players suggesting changes to tactics and strategies in the moment via direct messaging or texting. Why not leverage the back-channel to up your ally skills? Ask a trusted peer to message you when you could be a better ally, and offer to do the same for them.

Nithya Ruff, who leads the open source office at Comcast and is also on the board of the Linux Foundation, has just such a relationship with a male colleague. She messages him when she thinks he could be a better supporter of herself or other women in the room. Similarly, he alerts her if there are things she should pay attention to in Twitter conversations.

Ruff also sees the power in women being back-channel buddies for each other to perform sanity checks on meeting dynamics. "Am I reading this correctly?" or "Am I over-reacting?"

Wondering how you might nudge your colleagues and allies through a direct message or text? Here's what it might look like:

- "Dude, you forgot to give Miriam a shout-out in your project update."

- "Hey, Jasmin made the same point you just made earlier in the meeting. Give her credit."
- "Stop talking. It's time to listen."

One last thing

In the era of COVID safety precautions, many office workers and students have become intimately familiar with the ins and outs of virtual and online meetings. These proxies for in-person gatherings are now the default for many groups of colleagues, and they have their own set of norms and pitfalls.

When someone doesn't turn on their camera for a video meeting, I tend to joke, "Are you having a bad hair day?" It usually gets a laugh, followed by an explanation that their camera is on the fritz or they haven't showered yet.

Now, after reading an article titled "Working from Home While Black" in the *Harvard Business Review*, I realize I shouldn't be singling out anyone for keeping the camera off. As the authors Laura Morgan Roberts and Courtney L. McCluney wrote, "Black workers often strategically engage in code-switching — adjusting their speech, appearance, and behaviors to optimize the comfort of others with the hopes of receiving fair treatment, quality service, and opportunities."[78]

They go on to explain that with working from home, Black employees "are now literally broadcasting more of their identities from their personal living spaces." Plus, "when barbershops and hair salons closed, Black workers were vulnerable to harsher judgements associated with natural (i.e., not chemically altered) hairstyles."

In other words, they can no longer code-switch in the same way, and I shouldn't call them out for wanting to keep their camera off. Neither should you. If someone has their camera off, trust that they have a good reason, and skip the teasing.

Actions for Better Allies:
Amplify and Advocate in Meetings

In many organizations, much of the workday is spent in meetings. This means that ensuring the voices of members of underrepresented groups are heard and valued is essential to creating an inclusive work culture.

- Challenge yourself to notice and take action when interruptions happen in meetings.
- Cultivate a culture of credit: Encourage everyone around you to acknowledge the originator of ideas as often as possible.
- Be vigilant and push back on off-topic questions and showboating.
- Take note of how attendees arrange themselves in meeting rooms. Do what you can to mix up seating arrangements so your marginalized coworkers are in power positions.
- Ask a back-channel buddy to keep you accountable.
- Don't insist that people turn on their video cameras for virtual meetings.

7

OFFICE HOUSEWORK

A few years back, a tech company hired me to advise and coach the steering committee for their women's employee resource group. I remember attending one of their monthly meetings, which started with the chairperson reviewing a file on her laptop to figure out whose turn it was to take notes. (Turns out that at the beginning of the year, they had made a rotation schedule for note-taking and a few other administrative tasks.) When she announced that it was Brian's turn, the only male member of the committee announced, "I'm not really very good at taking notes, so someone else should do that."

I was taken aback, but not so much that I didn't think of something to say in the moment. In fact, I believe I had a spot-on response: "Practice makes perfect, and this is the perfect place to practice." There was no way I was going to let Brian get away with not doing his fair share of the meeting housework. Especially given the research on the topic.

What research, you ask? After Ellen Pao lost her gender discrimination lawsuit against Kleiner Perkins in 2015, a group of women decided to run a survey. They realized that while many women had similar stories to Pao's, most men were surprised and unaware of the issues facing women in the workplace. They decided to collect data as proof that discrimination happens across tech. After surveying hundreds of women with at least ten years of work experience, most of it in Silicon Valley, they published the results. Their report is called "The Elephant in the Valley." I mentioned it briefly in the previous chapter, and it's pretty telling.

One piece of data that surfaced in the final report: Almost half of the women surveyed (47 percent) had been asked to perform lower-level tasks that male colleagues had not been asked to do. In other words, they'd been asked to take on more office housework.[79] When the 3% Movement repeated this survey for the advertising industry, 60% of the women reported it had happened to them.[80]

Another research study found that women tend to volunteer for these "nonpromotable" tasks more than men; that women are more frequently asked to take such tasks on; and that when asked, they are more likely to say yes.[81] And research from the Center for WorkLife Law at the University of California, Hastings College of the Law, indicates that women of color are tasked with office housework even more frequently than their white colleagues.[82] This imbalance means that people who are saddled with food ordering, room cleanup, and other administrative duties that are not part of their job description may miss out on more visible, notable tasks and eventually be conceptualized as lower-level employees, even if they have high potential. Allies can change this dynamic. In fact, it's the responsibility of allies to change it.

Understanding office housework

Every workplace has office housework — tasks that need to get done but don't impact the bottom line. Chances are they don't lead to career growth; they may even impact it negatively. The most obvious example of office housework is taking the minutes at a meeting if that's not part of one's job description. (As a former program manager and epic notetaker, I know the value of good notes. I'm not diminishing this role at all. I'm simply calling it out as office housework if it's not part of a person's assigned responsibilities.)

There are many more examples. In fact, each time I coach women on how to rise above office housework, I learn about more ways it shows up. Here are some administrative and undervalued tasks that my clients have been asked to do that they don't see their male peers being tapped for.

Office Housework Tasks

Take the notes at a meeting and track action items.

Track down people who are late to a meeting.

Schedule the follow-up meeting.

Order food or make reservations at a restaurant.

Clean whiteboards and clear coffee mugs.

Plan a team-building event.

Join the hiring committee for another team.

Collect money for a gift for a coworker's new baby.

Be the only mentor for the interns, every summer.

If women accept these tasks when asked, they may be kept from the work they'll be evaluated on. If they refuse, they may be pegged as selfish or touchy. This issue is compounded for women of color. Caty, a manager at a technology company, told *Harvard Business Review*, "As a visibly Black woman in the workplace, I am often caught in a double-bind where if I don't accept the office housework, I'm considered an 'Angry Black' woman."[83]

Women are also often perceived as "enjoying" this work simply because they are more likely to do it. A few years ago, I taught a workshop at a software engineering school in San Francisco. The topic was how to be a better ally, and during the segment on office housework, one of the men in attendance asked, "But what if someone enjoys doing these tasks? Like Jess, who frequently washes mugs that are left in the sink? I think she enjoys cleaning up because it helps her handle stress." I then asked if Jess was also in the workshop. She was. And was it true that she enjoyed washing the mugs? She vehemently answered, "No." She did this task only because she hated seeing a sink full of mugs a lot more than she minded washing them.

Organizing baby showers for teammates or mentoring new employees may or may not be enjoyable for the person who takes on these responsibilities. It doesn't actually matter. Regardless of whether someone enjoys doing these tasks or not, there can be a negative impact. An impact on how they are perceived. An impact on the work they need to deliver. An impact on their career.

The impact of office housework

When we take on office housework, we move into a subservient role, which can lead to being seen as less valuable than our peers. When we volunteer to take notes or wash mugs, we look less leaderly in a culture that devalues these tasks. By spending time on housework tasks, we have less time to spend on more valued projects. On contributions that directly impact the business. On deliverables that count during performance appraisals. On work that creates visibility and leads to career growth.

In some cases, people from underrepresented groups are given work that's *adjacent* to visible or important assignments. For instance, a recent study of women lawyers found that 70 percent of those surveyed worked for firms where there were zero women — or just one token woman — sitting on powerful and influential compensation committees. The respondents also reported feeling that the committee work they *were* typically given — such as developing talent — did not do them any favors when annual reviews came around.[84] Different assignments might have bolstered their careers, but the ones they were handed simply dragged them down.

Office housework tasks can also interrupt flow. I heard from an engineer who loves babies and frequently offered to collect money to buy gifts for new parents on her team. Over time she started to regret it. Inevitably, she'd be hot on the trail of tracking down a gnarly coding bug when someone would stop by to chip in some money and sign the card, and stay for a few minutes to chat. It totally interrupted her flow, and she lost valuable time getting back to where she was.

Last but not least, those who are taking the meeting notes are often a step behind the conversation, documenting what has been said instead of making killer points themselves. By helping everyone else, they are putting themselves at a distinct disadvantage.

How to change office housework distribution

There are many ways in which allies can disrupt the norms around how office housework is handled. Depending on your position within a department or company, you can impact the distribution of this work using a variety of tactics:

- If you're part of a new committee or working group that's forming, recommend setting up a rotation schedule for any administrative tasks that aren't part of someone's job description. Think scheduling meetings, taking notes, timekeeping, and ordering food.

- If you're a supervisor, spread office housework tasks among your team. For example, if you notice one person is always tasked with mentoring the summer interns, say something like, "Ann's great at mentoring. But it's the perfect stretch assignment for Jacob, who's never done it before."

- If you're a manager or mentor and notice someone regularly volunteering for menial tasks, talk to them in private. Let them know you're concerned that the office housework they're taking on will affect their career growth. Encourage them to look for more impactful tasks to get involved with, and offer a few examples to nudge them in the right direction.

Here are some phrases that your mentees or direct reports can use when people ask them to do office housework:

- **"I'll have to ask my manager about prioritizing it."**
  Unless the person making the request *is* the manager, it can be helpful to postpone agreeing to office housework until after discussing it with a supervisor or boss. Their input will provide cover for saying no.

- **"I'd like to understand why you think I'm the right person to handle that."** Forcing someone to articulate specific talents or credentials related to ordering lunch or scheduling a meeting often makes them realize their own bias.

- **"Remember, I volunteered last time. Let's spread the wealth."** The person making the request may need reminding that they should distribute office housework more evenly among team members.

Regardless of your position, as in-person meetings break up, look around. If there are mugs, pastry boxes, or other post-meeting detritus left on the table, take a minute to throw out the trash and bring the rest to the nearest kitchen — especially if you're in a position of privilege or authority. Or point it out to someone walking out with you, and ask them to help out. If you don't, chances are the last woman to leave the room will feel compelled to clean up the mess.

If you have the ability to impact company policies, consider holding a meeting *about* office housework. You could facilitate a brainstorming session about which tasks qualify, discuss why it's detrimental to foist them on women and other marginalized employees, and identify approaches for disrupting how your team handles office housework.

There are many more ideas for effectively responding to inequitable requests in Ruchika Tulshyan's article, "Women of Color Get Asked to Do More 'Office Housework.' Here's How They Can Say No."[85] In preparation for your brainstorming session, consider circulating that article (and others on office housework) so attendees will have some background on the dynamics that will be discussed.

Relying on certain people or groups to handle tasks that don't drive business impact or lead to career growth is a prime example of unconscious bias. Most people who assume that women will do the office dishes don't even realize they're being chauvinistic until someone points it out. Allies can and should educate colleagues, helping to change how office housework is distributed and eradicating this erosive and harmful prejudice.

Actions for Better Allies:
Share the Load

Office housework isn't just aggravating. Calling exclusively on women, BIPOC, and members of other marginalized groups to perform it means preventing them from tackling more meaningful work. With that in mind:

- Share the work among the team. For example, if you notice one person is always tasked with mentoring the summer interns, say something like, "Ann's great at mentoring. But it's the perfect stretch assignment for Jacob, who has never done it before."
- Set up a rotation for tasks like taking minutes or scheduling the next meeting.
- If you're in a position of privilege or authority, model better behavior yourself by clearing the lunch leftovers or used coffee mugs, rather than assuming someone else will take care of it.
- Never assume that certain coworkers are shouldering office housework because they "enjoy" it or find it "rewarding."

8

EVERYDAY LANGUAGE

Language is powerful and, let's face it, shifts regularly to adapt to current events, trends, needs, and so forth. Words used in the past may no longer be the right ones to use today. They might go out of fashion, you might learn that they're not inclusive or harmful to others, or your own circumstances might change and affect what's appropriate or not. (For example, a parent decides to stop swearing in order to be a better role model for their child.)

I remember talking about language with my son Ted, and he mentioned that "to orient oneself" has roots in aligning two maps eastward, toward the "Orient." Not too long ago, it was widely accepted practice to refer to Asia as "the Orient" and the people who lived there as "Orientals." Today, that's no longer the case. Our language has shifted to use "Asia" and "Asians," which have been deemed to be more respectful. (It's unlikely that anyone of Asian descent would take offense if you talk about "orientation," but the root of the word is still one that's decidedly outdated.)

Here's another example of how language changes over time in response to social shifts.

Brad Johnson, a professor at the U.S. Naval Academy and coauthor of *Athena Rising* and *Good Guys,* told me he's seen many shifts away from inappropriate terms, especially because the ratio of women enrollees has doubled since he started teaching, from about 15 percent to about 30 percent. Years ago, Johnson would hear his students using the term *WUBA*, pronounced "woobah." He didn't know what it meant until someone finally explained it to him: "Women with Unbelievably Big Asses," an incredibly demeaning and derogatory thing to say. He says that the term has all but vanished from common use — and that, in fact, if that word were to be used at the Naval Academy today, there would be a swift, negative response from other men.

Although many people accept that language is fluid and impacted by social forces, others resist change. It can be aggravating to discover that words or phrases that were acceptable for decades are suddenly taboo. But those who push back are often the ones with the most privilege and the ones least likely to be insulted or harmed by the terms they refuse to give up. Those who resist change are also likely to have a narrow understanding of *why* a certain word or phrase is no longer acceptable. If they saw the big picture, they might be more willing to remove it from their vocabularies.

So, this chapter looks at a wide variety of problematic terms and word categories that imply bias, cause harm, or otherwise generate negative responses in workplaces. Many are related to gender, identity, or ethnicity, but others touch on other traits or differences. Allies can help build more inclusive and welcoming workplaces by avoiding particular words and remaining open to future shifts in language. Allies can also apologize when they discover they've been unwittingly using a problematic term.

Speaking of which, this chapter is far from comprehensive. There are plenty of other words that are part of everyday language that are no longer acceptable — words that allies should be aware of to be more inclusive, especially in common workplace situations. (For a fascinating look at other terms with unexpectedly racist roots — including moron and gypped — see the article "11 Common English Words And Phrases With Racist Origins" on *www.babbel.com*.)

Being an ally is a journey, and part of that journey is being attuned to the ever-changing needs of those around us. That includes adjusting our everyday language. Let's explore a few terms and word groups that allies should avoid, and examine why they've fallen out of favor. I've curated this guidance from experts and other helpful sources, which are listed in the "Additional Resources" section later in this book.

Gendered language

Allies should always be on the lookout for unnecessarily gendered language. When it comes to modifying titles or roles, consider what value, if any, is added by including a gender term at all. Why say "female lawyer" when "lawyer" would do just fine? Why reinforce nursing as "women's work" by saying "male nurse" and implying that it's odd or unusual for a man to work in that field?

Allies working in male-dominated industries should be on the lookout for "man" terms that imply other genders aren't expected or welcome. I remember when it was common to estimate projects in terms of "man-hours" — and some people still do. Sure, there were more men working on these projects than women, but it was easy enough to start using the gender-neutral "work-hours" or, for software projects, "dev-hours."

Deb Liu, who has worked as vice president of marketplace at Facebook, believes that gendered language of all kinds can be harmful in the workplace. She writes:

> Once I started documenting these words, I heard them everywhere — in meetings, hallway conversations and presentations. Many of the masculine phrases like "manpower" and "right-hand man" were neutral to positive, usually indicating a position of strength while nearly all of the feminine ones, like "prima donna" and "Debbie downer" were negative and indicated weakness. These subtle sexist messages are all around us, and as a mother of a boy and two girls, I wonder what it says to them about the world we live in. If someone says a project is a "two-man job," who comes to mind for the opportunity? ... The best way to confront unconscious bias is to force ourselves to be aware of how it is present all around us, even built directly into [the] work lexicon we use every day.[86]

Liu's story reminds me of something my daughter Emma experienced when studying computer science in college. One of her coding assignments included the encouraging note, "Man up and edit the stencil code. You can do it!" Then there's the first full-time job offer my son received after graduating from college in 2020: draftsman at an architecture firm. Once you start paying attention to "man" phrases, you'll notice how commonplace they are.

Because we live in a world where gender is a spectrum and professions aren't limited by gender, allies can do the most good by using and promoting gender-neutral terms. Be particularly mindful of the following examples.

Guys

Many people use the word *guys* to refer to a mixed-gender group. I have to admit I've done so a lot, both when talking to my family ("Hey guys, dinner is ready") and in professional settings ("Alright guys, let's wrap up this meeting"). And I can't even begin to count how many times I must have said "hey yous guys" as a kid growing up in Rhode Island. (Fortunately, I broke myself of that habit a while ago.)

"But wait," you might be thinking, "*guys* is gender-neutral. After all, that's how everyone uses it. Plus, it's been that way for years." You might even ask some women coworkers or friends and hear that they are perfectly fine with the term.

Well, it may be fine for many, but not for all. Imagine you're a woman or a nonbinary individual and need to use a restroom in a coffee shop. You find a door marked "guys." Would you go in, or would you look around for another option?

Or imagine you're a straight, cisgender man. How would you answer the question, "How many guys did you date in high school and college?"

Maybe "guys" isn't as gender-neutral as you thought.

My friend Anne Janzer, a writing expert and author of *Get the Word Out*, points out that subtleties in language may seem minor when called out, but their collective power is formidable. If you don't identify as male, yet you get addressed as "you guys" over and over again, it can feel like an erasure of your gender identity. This is especially true for transgender people, who may already feel that their gender identities are questioned or rejected by the people around them.

"You might argue that people are too sensitive to this stuff. Perhaps that's true, but this sensitivity may not rise to the level of consciousness," Janzer explains. "It may show up as a background discomfort, or an intuition that something isn't a good fit. If you're writing or speaking and want to attract a larger audience, you don't want to turn people away inadvertently. Your word choices may be metaphorically slamming doors in your readers' faces, telling them they're not welcome."[87]

I've been doing my best to stop using "guys" for a group that isn't all men. I want to be more inclusive of other genders, and I certainly don't want to give the impression that men are the preferred gender. Sure, it slips out every now and then, and when it does, I'll say something like, "Whoops, I meant to say 'folks.'" Or "friends" or "people" or "humans" or "y'all" or some other nongendered word. Want more options? Check out Kim Z. Dale's article "40 Gender-Neutral Alternatives to Saying 'You Guys'," which includes great alternatives like "crew," "squad," and "cohort."[88]

Ladies and gentlemen

The age-old phrase, "Welcome, ladies and gentlemen," also needs a facelift. It's not inclusive of everyone in the room because it fails to acknowledge people who are nonbinary. Even if you know that every person in the room is cisgender, there's no reason to adhere to exclusive language. It's a good practice to always default to the most unbiased phrasing possible. So instead of "ladies and gentlemen," try using "distinguished guests" or a simple "good morning/good afternoon everyone," like the London Tube announcers started using in 2017.[89]

Speaking of "ladies," that word can come across as patronizing for a number of reasons. Because "lady" is still related to nobility in some cultures, it can make modern women feel as though they're being reminded of a time when women were quieter, gentler, and more "well-behaved." The male equivalent is "gentleman," but aside from messages of welcome, this word has largely dropped from common usage. (Ever heard someone shout, "Hey, watch it, gentleman"? Me neither.) The derivative "ladylike" also hearkens back to less equitable times when women behaved in a certain demure way, and it reinforces the false gender binary. Finally, "lady" has become a condescending prefix to jobs or activities that are associated with male culture: lady cop, lady umpire, lady politician.[90] Even though you may hear women calling each other "ladies" or even "gals" or "girls," I recommend that allies say "women." It's more respectful.

Reclaimed and reappropriated language

Perhaps you've heard lesbians refer to themselves as dykes, people from rural areas call themselves rednecks, or women of Asian descent deem themselves tiger moms. Maybe you've heard rap songs by Black artists who use the n-word. There is a long history of oppressed races, groups, and classes twisting the slurs that have been formulated to demean them. The act of reappropriating a slur can be confusing and painful, but it can have positive repercussions.

James L. Gibson, a professor of government at Washington University, coauthored a 2019 study examining language reappropriation. He and his colleagues found that context is crucial, but under some circumstances, reclaimed slurs can actually become neutral or even positive.

"When a group is seen as taking control of a historically disparaging term, it can indeed neutralize the insulting content of the term," Gibson says. "And it does so among the group that is the target of the insult, as well as among members of the majority group. Reappropriation does seem to work in the sense of defusing insults, rendering them less disparaging and harmful."[91]

So, if these historically negative terms have been reclaimed by the populations they describe, are they fair game for everyone to use?

Probably not. Reappropriation creates solidarity within the group doing the reappropriating, but people outside of the group should assume those loaded terms are still taboo.

If you aren't sure what's off-limits, follow this advice from Jeannie Gainsburg, author of *The Savvy Ally*: "Hey, I heard you use the term _____ earlier. I want to make sure I'm being respectful. Is that an okay term for me to use too, or should I avoid it?"[92]

Pronouns

For a long time, "he" was considered the default pronoun in the English language to refer to a single person. It took decades of effort for feminists to shift this standard by advocating for the use of "he or she" and "her or his," but many people still use "he" on occasion even if they don't know the gender of the person to whom they're referring. Doing so perpetuates bias. For example, imagine attending a hiring committee meeting for a software engineer position and hearing someone say, "When the candidate arrives, he should first meet with ___." The person is probably thinking about the mostly male job applicant pool for the role and reinforcing this stereotype by using the pronoun "he."

To circumvent this implicit gender bias and the awkwardness of saying "he or she," it's fine to use "them" and "they," even when talking about an individual person. The grammatically minded among us (including me) might find this awkward initially, but over time it becomes more familiar and natural. I'm now fine hearing (or saying), "When the candidate arrives, they should first meet with ___." In fact, I've even intentionally written this book using "they" and "them" in this way. (If your inner grammarian continues to resist, remember that revered writers including William Shakespeare and Jane Austen used "they" as a singular pronoun.[93])

In addition to employing "they" when a person's gender identity is uncertain, it's helpful to make yourself aware of the language someone uses to refer to themself. Many nonbinary people use "them" and "they." There are plenty of people, whether cisgender, trans, or nonbinary, for whom it is impossible to know what pronouns to use just by looking at them. Even some cisgender people forsake the traditional "he" or "she" pronouns for "they" or something else. It's presumptive to assign someone a pronoun based on their physical appearance.

Not sure what pronouns to use? As I learned from my friend Dom Brassey, when meeting someone new, introducing yourself with a simple "I use 'she' and 'her.' What pronouns do you use?" is respectful, and their answer gives us clear guidance. If you don't want to ask, you can always just use "they" until you learn more.

And remember that if you are a cisgendered ally, clarifying your pronouns is a simple but powerful act of support. Whether you do this verbally or in an email signature, on a nametag, or as part of your video conference profile, you are helping to normalize the practice of sharing pronouns. This is helpful to genderfluid, transgender, and other nonbinary folks, who get loads of pushback on the pronoun issue overall. Sinclair Sexsmith, a writer and nonbinary person, tweeted on this subject, saying:[94]

Sinclair Sexsmith @MrSexsmith · Mar 31, 2019   °°°

Dear cis people who put your pronouns on your "hello my name is" nametags:

Thank you.

When you do that, I feel more comfortable putting they/them.

And I feel much more comfortable talking to you, bc you already tell me you know a little about the gender binary.

Love,
me

 ♡ 45   ⇄ 429   ♡ 1.9K   ↑

Finally, please don't ask someone for their "preferred" pronouns. That makes it sound like using their pronouns is optional, which it's not.

Names

I tend to mispronounce names that I'm not familiar with. While this may not seem like a big deal, it can be one more reminder to someone that they are different from the norm. It might make someone feel they don't belong or that they're less important than others in a meeting. In a *Harvard Business Review* article titled "If You Don't Know How to Say Someone's Name, Just Ask," inclusion strategist Ruchika Tulshyan wrote,

> Learning to pronounce a colleague's name correctly is not just a common courtesy but it's an important effort in creating an inclusive workplace, one that emphasizes psychological safety and belonging.[95]

Tulshyan cited a 2012 study that reported when students of color had their names mispronounced in the classroom, it affected their social emotional well-being and, by extension, harmed their ability to learn. The study also concluded that mispronouncing the names of students of color constituted a racial microaggression because it created shame and disassociation from their culture. Both of these findings port over into the workplace, as you can imagine.[96]

I know it's important to get it right, but some names are hard for me. For many years, every time I met someone who worked at LinkedIn, I told them about my dream feature: Allow users to record their names so others can hear how to pronounce them. This would be a game-changer for me. I could listen to someone's name before meeting them or as a follow-up to a conversation so I could get it right the next time. (In my pitch, I also mentioned that it would increase page views and usage of the platform. This feature would be good for business, too.)

Imagine how thrilled I was when I read that LinkedIn decided to roll out this exact feature in 2020. Fantastic!

Even if you think your name is easy to say, take the time to record your pronunciation. There may be people who aren't familiar with your name and will want to address you correctly. Plus, doing so can normalize using this profile feature.

Of course, we can't always rely on LinkedIn to help us out. Sometimes we need name-pronunciation hacks we can use in real time. In an article for KQED, reporter Gail Cornwall shared tips collected from educators for remembering students' names. Things like:

- Tell someone, "I don't know how to say your name yet, can you explain it to me? I'm working on learning it, and it's important to me to say it the way it's meant to be said."
- Keep saying it until you get it right.
- Use names as much as possible, almost as obnoxiously as a telemarketer would, until they sink in.[97]

She also shared what may be a secret weapon for those of us who find it challenging to pronounce unfamiliar names: *www.pronouncenames.com*. It's a super helpful site. If you struggle like I do, bookmark it now.

And please, don't make up nicknames for someone who's name is hard for you to remember. Show them you respect them enough to learn their full name. In *The Savvy Ally*, Jeannie Gainsburg states a reason for this that ought to be obvious: We should all learn to refer to people in the ways they want to be referred to.

Yet, for transgender people, there may be some nuances to keep in mind. As Gainsburg wrote,

> I have worked with many transgender coworkers. Some had
> legally changed their names and some had not. It did not
> matter to me as their coworker. I used their current name. I
> never asked what their name used to be or, even worse, what
> their 'real' name was. (Hint: This is rude.)[98]

She goes on to advise avoiding any mental gymnastics as we talk about someone's past and consider using their former name. Steer clear of, "Hey Alice, when you were Alfred, did you play on any sports teams?" Don't out them or call attention to their past. Just stick to their current name.

If you're thinking that's easy enough, read on.

There are organizations that insist on using employees' legal names on badges, email addresses, video conference accounts, and other internal systems. Yet, not all transgender people legally change their name. It can be expensive, it may require a judge's approval (and not all judges support people transitioning to another gender), and it may require a notice to be published in a newspaper, which might lead to safety concerns. So, if your company requires legal names to be used, please advocate for change. Ask if current names can be added to these systems and be displayed in lieu of legal names.

MasterCard recently took a step toward supporting transgender and nonbinary customers' name needs by rolling out a "True Name" program. As reported in the *Washington Post*, "Cardholders will soon be able to swap out credit, debit or prepaid cards with their 'dead name' with new ones featuring the names they actually use. Experts say it's a first for the financial services industry."[99]

Hopefully, it will not be the last.

Finally, bear in mind that mixing up the only two Black or Latinx workers in your office isn't just dismissive, it's racist. In a *Washington Post* article titled, "Co-workers keep mixing up people of color in the office. It's more than a mistake," reporter Rachel Hatzipanagos shared this anecdote:

> It happened again. Nicholas Pilapil got an email clearly meant for his co-worker, Jonathan Castanien. Previously, Pilapil had missed a meeting invitation because their white co-workers couldn't tell them apart. So they came up with a cheeky way to address the problem. Between their desks, Pilapil and Castanien hung a sign that read, "This company has worked __ days without an incident. Incorrect names are avoidable."
>
> Whenever a co-worker called one by the other's name, they would reset the count to zero. During the six months or so that the sign was up, the count never exceeded 14 days, Pilapil said. In total, they were misidentified about 50 times.
>
> Pilapil called Castanien his "work twin" — sarcastically, because they bear only a passing resemblance to each other. Aside from being in their 20s, they don't share many characteristics: Pilapil is Filipino, has fuller lips, a squarer jaw and a darker complexion than Castanien, who is Vietnamese, Chinese and German.[100]

There are so many reasons to learn to correctly identify and name your colleagues, but the most important one is to show them that you see them, respect them, and value them. Period.

Disability as a negative metaphor

Some of the most common and prominent problematic terms refer to gender or ethnicity, but there are important examples that disparage people who are disabled or have mental health conditions. This includes those whose conditions or disabilities may be invisible to the naked eye.

During a diversity and inclusion webinar I attended in 2018, one of the speakers surprised me with her less-than-inclusive language. Specifically, she used "nuts" and "crazy" to describe unusual business conditions. My concern? Using these terms in casual conversation can diminish the experience of people who live with mental health conditions. (It's similar to how I wouldn't use "retarded" as a synonym for "stupid" or "nonsensical.")

Instead of "crazy," here are some alternatives to consider: "unusual," "outrageous," "surprising," "wild," or even "unprecedented."

Along related lines, calling something "lame" when you find it to be subpar is disrespectful to people with physical disabilities. The term was coined hundreds of years ago to describe animals and people with injuries, but is now used to describe anything that isn't performing to standard.[101] This new, more liberal application implies that disabled people are themselves disappointing. Understandably, people with disabilities often object to having their collective identity used as the default proxy for virtually anything negative. Instead of "lame," try "mediocre," "unsatisfying," "meager," or terms I've used here, such as "subpar" or "disappointing."

There are many more examples of such linguistic microaggressions. In "Doing Social Justice: Thoughts on Ableist Language and Why It Matters," graduate student Rachel Cohen-Rottenberg wrote:

> Disability metaphors abound in our culture, and they exist almost entirely as pejoratives. You see something wrong? Compare it to a disabled body or mind: Paralyzed. Lame. Crippled. Schizophrenic. Diseased. Sick. Want to launch an insult? The words are seemingly endless: Deaf. Dumb. Blind. Idiot. Moron. Imbecile. Crazy. Insane. Retard. Lunatic. Psycho. Spaz.[102]

Once you become attuned to these words and phrases, you'll notice them everywhere. For instance, in everyday conversation, having a "blind spot" tends to imply something negative. As in, if someone were better or more skilled, they wouldn't have the blind spot (e.g., "You appear to have a blind spot to this emerging competitive threat," or "Because of your blind spot, you missed an opportunity").

Because of this negative connotation, the phrase "blind spot" may be offensive to people with blindness. Instead, why not describe the person as "being unaware" or substitute the phrase "blank spot"?

To learn about alternatives to these metaphors, check out the comprehensive "Ableism/Language" list compiled by disability justice advocate Lydia X. Z. Brown.[103]

Language that disrespects Indigenous peoples

Not too long ago, I used the word "powwow" to refer to a group discussion I was about to facilitate. As the word came out of my mouth, I realized I should have chosen a different one. One that would be more inclusive and respectful of Native Americans and their heritage. Many nations still hold powwows to gather and celebrate, and none of them take place in corporate conference rooms.[104] Even if this weren't a term that was still in active use, it describes a specific type of event that honors a specific population, so appropriating it is insulting.

My friend Michelle Glauser — founder of Techtonica and creator of the Bay Area's 2015 #ILookLikeAnEngineer ad campaign — offers a slew of alternatives, including "meeting," "check-in," "talk," and "one-on-one."[105] Right on.

There are plenty of other sayings that diminish or disparage the culture of Indigenous peoples. Examples include "going off the reservation," "lowest person on the totem pole," "too many chiefs, not enough Indians," and "Indian giver."[106] Let's stay away from all of them.

Some organizations are already moving in this direction. In August 2020, former Winter Olympics site Squaw Creek announced they would change their name. As reported in the

Mercury News, "The word 'squaw,' derived from the Algonquin language, may have once simply meant 'woman,' but over generations, the word morphed into a misogynist and racist term to disparage indigenous women."[107] The Washington Redskins NFL team became just the Washington Football Team while they search for a new mascot. Land O' Lakes butter no longer uses an image of a Native American woman on its packaging. It's encouraging to see a wide variety of organizations acknowledging their past slights to Indigenous cultures, even if that acknowledgment feels long overdue.

Back in Chapter 1, I told you about a white software engineer who, when asked to name her "spirit animal" as part of a team-building exercise, pushed back. She didn't want to take part in the cultural appropriation of Native American spiritual practices. Here's a nifty alternative I learned from Aubrey Blanche, director of equitable design and impact at Culture Amp: Use "patronus" instead. If you don't want to reference the Harry Potter books, you could simply ask "What's your favorite animal?"

Popular industry terms

During my long career working in tech, I know I've used many noninclusive or outright harmful words and phrases, including "master/slave" to describe storage backup systems and "whitelist/blacklist" to filter items in algorithms. Despite their racist undertones, these terms are industry-standard and almost universally accepted. While it can be challenging to steer colleagues away from jargon and terms that have been widely used in their fields for decades, allies must focus on doing what's right instead of what's easy. And that includes eradicating insider language and shorthand terms that are problematic.

Here are a few more examples from various industries:

- In policy and law, situations that are exempt from a new rule are referred to as being "grandfathered in." This phrase is related to poll taxes and literacy tests some states used to prevent Black men from voting. While these states couldn't ban Black men from voting, they could make it difficult. And they used a "grandfather clause" exempting white people from the taxes and tests if their ancestors had the right to vote before the Civil War. This phrase is still popular today. Why not use "exempt" instead?
- Electrical components are often labeled as "male/female" parts. Why not use "pin/socket" or "plug/receptacle" instead?
- Many scientists and researchers use the term "blind" when referring to their research. Terms like "blind review" and "double-blind randomized controlled trial" are common. Why not say "masked" instead?
- In the publishing industry, a "dummy" describes an early layout mock-up with stand-in images. "Dummy" is also a slur for people who can't speak. Why not say "mock-up" instead?

Often changes in industry terms or company-specific words come from leadership. A few years ago, I attended a panel where Michael Lopp, then vice president of engineering at Pinterest, mentioned his goal of using more inclusive language. In addition to steering clear of "guys" to refer to mixed-gender groups, he shared one other example. He'd started using "straw dog" as an alternative to "straw man" when talking about rough proposals. I'm betting the unexpected word choice caught people by surprise and encouraged them to examine their language choices.

That said, changes can also come from collegial discussion. Security Nerdette launched a Twitter thread suggesting that programmers use "safelist/blocklist" instead of "whitelist/blacklist" and a fascinating discussion ensued. While some respondents insisted that the colors white and black were neutral in this context, others pointed out that the present-day effect (reinforcing unconscious racial bias) is more important than the origin (the 1600s and unrelated to race). Other tech experts chimed in with other ideas for term swaps, including replacing "master/slave" with "primary/replica." Many committed to making these changes in their own workplaces.[108]

To continue learning about using more inclusive language in your own workplace, make a "language matters" channel on your corporate Slack or other discussion tool. Health-care tech company Nuna has such a channel for coworkers to ask questions about noninclusive language and suggest alternatives. The company also uses it to discuss effective ways to point out when someone uses problematic language and for staff to learn how to respond when called out for their own language choices.[109]

As your workplace identifies language you want to "retire," consider using a tool to automatically flag noninclusive words and phrases and make alternate suggestions. I belong to a cross-company tech leadership Slack group with a Slackbot that looks for "guys," "crazy," "insane," "midget," "pimp," "has balls," and other such terms and replies automatically with an explanation of why the word or phrase isn't inclusive and some alternatives to consider. It's definitely effective. (In the "Additional Resources" section at the end of the book, you'll find an open source link you can use to create such a Slackbot for your company.)

Titles and honorifics

In 2018, across social media, women with PhDs started adding "Dr." to their profile names to claim their hard-earned achievement and push back in solidarity against trolls who were calling them "arrogant," "immodest," or "vain" for doing so.

It all started with a tweet by Dr. Jensen Moore:[110]

Dr. Jensen Moore @MagicalPR · Jun 17, 2018   ○○○
Added Dr. to my Twitter name today. Always felt I shouldn't because I'd been married to a "real" doctor (orthopedic surgeon). So I was just the "paper Dr." But I worked 3 jobs to put him through medical school WHILE getting my Ph.D. and having our 2 kids. So #ImmodestWomen it is.

♡ 592   ↱ 2.3K   ♡ 30.3K   ↑

Can you imagine a man getting flak for insisting that people use the right honorific when addressing him? Or calling him "vain" for referring to himself as Dr.? Recognizing this double standard, hundreds of women responded, many of them by adding Dr. to their own handles. I love that they used the #ImmodestWomen hashtag to draw attention to the issue. You know what else? I love that "Dr." is a gender-neutral title.

Fast forward to December 2020, and this topic is still being debated. The *Wall Street Journal* published an opinion piece stating that Dr. Jill Biden, who earned a doctorate in education, should think about dropping the honorific as First Lady of the United States. Why? The author claimed that it "feels fraudulent, even comic."[111]

Let's support every person from a marginalized group who decides to be confident, authoritative, and proud of their hard-earned achievements — whether by claiming their credentials in their social media profiles or with some other action.

Unconscious demotions

In Chapters 4 and 5, I discussed the dangers of assuming that someone holds a particular type of role based on their age, gender, or race. This type of inference is called an "unconscious demotion." In June 2018, professor Marisa Franco tweeted:[112]

> **Marisa Franco** @DrMarisaGFranco · Aug 14, 2018
> Tip: Instead of asking unfamiliar faces in your department "are you a student?" ask "what is your role, here?" This helps folks who haven't traditionally been the face of academia-- young professors, professors of color, female professors in mostly male departments --belong.
> 234 8.5K 36.5K

In tech, this might look like someone asking, "Are you an intern?" or "Do you work in marketing or HR?" (As I said in Chapter 5, while there's nothing wrong with those disciplines, this kind of assumption can be another signal to marginalized engineers that they don't belong.) On a movie set, this might look like someone asking "Are you a production assistant?" or "Can you get me a coffee, dear?"

To be more inclusive, follow Dr. Suzanne Wertheim's advice: Don't give an "unconscious demotion" by articulating that you think someone is in a position lower or less technical than their real position. Instead, ask an open-ended question.[113]

> **Dr. Suzanne Wertheim is feeling relieved** @Worth... · Aug 15, 2018
> It's one of the most basic ways to avoid giving an unconscious demotion.
>
> Ask an open-ended question instead of articulating that you think someone is in a position lower than their real position.
>
> (Being on the receiving end of an unconscious demotion can feel awful.)

One last thing

Allies can play an important role by being role models for more inclusive language. At the Naval Academy, Brad Johnson told me that he believes internal language has shifted because senior leaders have made it a priority to use more inclusive language themselves. Also, there's an expectation that the men will police each other, because women are still the minority group. Sounds like a best practice for workplaces everywhere.

Actions for Better Allies:
Watch Your Words

As Security Nerdette pointed out in her Twitter thread, "How we spend our day is how we spend our life."[114] It may seem like word choice is a minor issue, but it's one that accumulates over time.

- Be aware and respectful of pronouns, gendered language, and phrases that are demeaning or offensive. Lead by example in how you use (or don't use) both.
- Take time to learn people's names and how to pronounce them.
- Create a safe space for people in your workplace or industry to ask questions and discuss problematic language.
- Be aware that some terms you think are innocuous may be harmful to others. If you mess up, apologize.

PART THREE

INCREASING
YOUR
IMPACT

9

ON STAGE

Back in 2012, when I started my coaching business, I have to admit that I floundered a bit. I had always worked for organizations that provided me with regular paychecks. I had zero experience creating a new business from scratch. So, I sought out advice from other coaches, independent contractors, and members of the women-in-tech community.

One recurring theme I heard was to get out and speak in public. To talk about my experience being a woman in the tech industry. To share my leadership stories. To become more visible. People told me it was a surefire way to start attracting coaching clients. Seems straightforward enough, right?

But here's the thing. While I had done some public speaking in the past — giving the occasional talk at a conference and leading my all-hands meetings as an executive — I didn't think I was good at it. Like most people, nerves got the best of me. I certainly didn't *enjoy* giving talks. And I really, really didn't want to do more of it.

Yet I embraced the advice because I realized it could be the key to growing my new business. So, I set a goal for myself: Scary as it might be, I was going to speak in public once a month. Since then, I've met or exceeded that goal. In my busiest month, I spoke ten times. And get this: I've come to love public speaking.

In fact, I'm now a self-proclaimed public speaking geek. I've even coauthored a book on the topic, *Present! A Techie's Guide to Public Speaking*, with Poornima Vijayashanker, to help others learn this craft. I especially want to see more people from underrepresented groups giving talks at all-hands meetings at their companies, at local events, and on stage at larger industry conferences.

After all, public speaking is like a career multivitamin. Presenting at a team meeting, a company gathering, or an external event increases one's visibility. Which leads to sponsors taking notice. And that leads to career growth.

Of course, there's one additional benefit. By simply being more visible, speakers become role models for others who may be just a step or two behind them on their own career journeys. When newer, younger, or less experienced employees see people who look like them speaking, it empowers them to follow suit. Plus, when they're a member of an underrepresented group, they get to bust stereotypes about what a leader or expert looks like.

This is why I encourage allies to help people from underrepresented backgrounds do more public speaking. Here's what that might look like:

- During Q&A sessions at your all-hands meetings or external events, take the first question from someone from an underrepresented group.
- Ask staff from marginalized groups to deliver project updates at team meetings.

- Introduce them to conference organizers who are putting together panels or looking for speakers.
- Attend their dry runs as they practice their presentations, to show support and give them feedback so they can improve.
- If you're asked to do a keynote or speak on a panel, pass the opportunity along to someone on your team or in your network who's from an underrepresented group.
- Turn your keynote into a showcase, like Megan Smith (then CTO of the United States) did at the 2015 Grace Hopper Celebration. Instead of delivering the keynote herself, she asked six women colleagues from the U.S. Digital Service to join her on stage to share the work they were doing.[115]

Taking any of these actions will make you a better ally. But there's much more that allies can do to influence public speaking opportunities in a variety of settings. Let's explore them.

Homogeneous speaker lineups

In the not-so-distant past, some clever person coined the term "manel" to describe a panel consisting of only men. A panel that subconsciously reinforces that men are the experts; that women don't belong. And then there are "manferences" — conferences that feature all-male speaker lineups. Another huge and ever-growing problem is the all-white panel, or "wanel." Across industries, these exclusionary events have become an epidemic.

Even more problematic is when these speakers don't have direct lived experience with the topic. Consider panels about the challenges faced by women in tech featuring only men. Or discussions on transgender rights where all the panelists are cisgender people. Or interfaith panels with speakers who represent different Christian denominations but no other world religions.

As a panel organizer myself, I can see how easy it is to select a homogeneous group. Most organizers reach out to their network to find people who can speak on the topic. If they lack diversity in their network (which most people do, as we learned in Chapter 4), chances are they're going to lack diversity at the event. However, ensuring that speakers represent a variety of viewpoints and experiences should be a stretch goal for allies. It might be challenging, but it's important enough that all allies should be willing to move outside their comfort zones to make it happen.

Here's an example from my own career: Back when I was a vice president at Adobe, I was a member of our Engineering Council, a group of senior technical leaders across the company. One of our initiatives was sponsoring an annual internal technical conference. Typically, we tapped two principal scientists to lead the yearly event, and they, in turn, would tap colleagues to run the various content tracks and review proposals from employees who wanted to speak.

One year, the two organizers (both white men) came to the Engineering Council with an update on their planning work. One of them announced, "We're proud of the diversity we've achieved with our committee. We have someone from each of Adobe's global offices." As he showed a slide with the employees' photos (all of whom were men), I quickly quipped, "I'm glad you've focused on diversity, but where are the women?" To their credit, they quickly admitted their mistake and sheepishly explained that they didn't know who to ask. I offered to help identify some women track chairs. This was important to me, because I believed the women track chairs would advocate for speaker diversity. And I was willing to create some public discomfort to ensure that the lineup was more inclusive.

More recently, I saw this tweet from Dr. Renzo Guinto:[116]

> **Renzo Guinto** @RenzoGuinto · Mar 30   ooo
> Just declined an invite to speak in a #COVID19 webinar when I learned
> that there is no single woman in a panel of 8 men (I will be 9th). Even in
> crisis time, & especially in this time, we must remain consistent with our
> convictions. #NoToManels #WomeninGlobalHealth #MaleAllyship
>
> ♡ 738   ↺ 2.5K   ♡ 19K   ↑

Virtual panels need representation just as much as in-person panels, and saying no to all-male panels (or all-white panels) is just one way to "remain consistent with our convictions." I, along with tens of thousands of people on Twitter, applauded Guinto's decision.

How else can you help if you're an ally? Here's another story that might offer some inspiration.

In April 2018, automation-in-testing advocate Richard Bradshaw showed his true colors as an ally. Upon discovering that the Code Europe conference he'd agreed to speak at had lined up only male speakers (a whopping eighty-seven of them), he promptly canceled. Bradshaw then went on to create a "speaker rider" for himself that requires both a code of conduct and diverse speakers for any event at which he'll agree to present.

Now *that's* saying "Not cool" with some stake in the game.

I encourage all allies reading this book to follow Bradshaw's example. Before accepting a speaking engagement or panel slot, do the same type of vetting discussed back in Chapter 5 when we examined organizing and attending events. Events at which you speak should be held to the same standards, so do some preliminary digging. Does the event website show only white men, or is there a diverse group of people represented? Is there a posted code of conduct? If all signs point to an exclusionary event, ask the organizers for clarification. Questions like "Will there be any speakers or panelists of color?" or "Are you planning to have a code of conduct?" let the hosts know where your priorities lie. Your inquiries may even prompt the organizers to make meaningful changes to their policies.

Refusing to sit on all-male or all-white panels is a simple way for allies to express their desire to see this change. Allies who want members of underrepresented groups to do more public speaking must be willing to move aside and point the spotlight at people with less privilege and access. Effective allies lead by example.

Now, sometimes "leading by example" is code for "avoiding conflict," but when it comes to being an ally, the behaviors we model can have a noticeable ripple effect. After Bradshaw canceled his appearance at Code Europe, he tweeted about it and wrote a follow-up blog post, in which he said:

> How did I let this happen? Your name was on that conference page Richard, your company was on that page! I felt embarrassed. These thoughts came after cancelling my attendance, cancelling was a must, as a male speaker who cares about their craft, cares about inclusion, there was only one option, the right one. It was great to read a few replies later from some of the other male speakers cancelling their attendance.[117]

Simply seeing Bradshaw announce his cancellation prompted other male panelists to follow suit. Just imagine the domino effect if more male allies did the same.

If you're a speaker or event organizer, here are some ally actions to take:

- **If you are asked to speak,** ask the organizer who else will be speaking on the panel or at the event. Review the list of speakers, if possible. If you see only people who look like you, push back like Richard Bradshaw did.

- **If you are an active public speaker,** refer colleagues from marginalized groups for the next request you get. Adam Singer, an analytics advocate at Google, had been giving about 25 talks each year, and in 2017 he decided to pass opportunities along to people he called "new voices." As a result, many of them became regulars on the speaking circuit.[118]
- **If you unexpectedly find yourself on a homogenous panel,** consider giving up your spot in the moment.
- **If you're organizing an event,** ask every male you're inviting to speak to recommend a woman, a person of color, or a member of another underrepresented group to also speak. And, as I recommended back in Chapter 1, take actions to diversify your network so you have a more varied group of people to tap for your next event.

Of course, panels and conferences aren't the only events where underrepresented voices should be amplified. Any gathering or meeting should be seen as a forum for diverse perspectives. And these principles can be applied to other kinds of inclusiveness. Everyone of any identity can ask whether BIPOC, women, transgender, nonbinary, and/or disabled speakers will be featured, and they can push back if not. When we create more opportunities for members of marginalized groups to speak, even if it means keeping quiet ourselves, we are enabling equity on multiple levels.

Asking about the code of conduct

In Chapter 5, I discussed the importance of creating and enforcing codes of conduct, and the concept resurfaces when it comes to discussing the need to screen speaking engagements. Here's your gentle reminder to ask about an event's code of conduct before agreeing to deliver a presentation or sit on a panel.

After accepting a speaking gig

Of course, there are plenty of times when allies can and should speak. Whenever you serve as a speaker, you can be an effective ally by making sure that your presentations are inclusive and accessible to all.

For instance, Matt May, accessibility expert and head of inclusive design at Adobe, tweeted the following:[119]

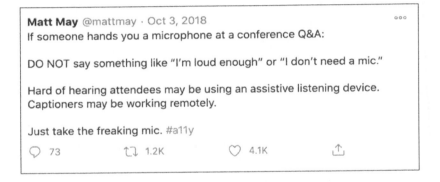

Matt May @mattmay · Oct 3, 2018

If someone hands you a microphone at a conference Q&A:

DO NOT say something like "I'm loud enough" or "I don't need a mic."

Hard of hearing attendees may be using an assistive listening device. Captioners may be working remotely.

Just take the freaking mic. #a11y

💬 73   🔁 1.2K   ♡ 4.1K   ⬆️

May made an important point, and one that many speakers don't consider while running a Q&A session. It's also important to avoid using tiny fonts in presentation slides, so all audience members can see the content, and to create visuals that are diverse and welcoming. (More on slide design in the next section.)

Ally actions don't stop with accessibility. When speakers with particular privileges or power are given the opportunity to address diverse audiences, it's their responsibility to be fully present and respectful.

Kat Gordon is the founder of the 3% Movement, whose mission is to change the ratio of women creative directors from

3 percent to 50 percent. (You may remember their research from Chapter 7.) In June 2015, it hosted an event in London that included a "Manbassadors" panel where four men from the creative industry spoke about their commitment to diversity. Sounds pretty good, right? Well…

They showed up, bragged on stage, and immediately left to go to the hotel bar and drink together. They didn't listen to other speakers. They didn't take the opportunity to learn about the challenges facing women in their field. They didn't diversify their networks.

Gordon was busy leading the event and didn't notice their absence. But if she had, she would have sent one of the good men who stuck around down to the bar to ask the other guys to embody true manbassadorship and come back to the event.

Even when allies can't or don't pass a speaking opportunity along to someone with less privilege or access, they can still comport themselves in ways that broadcast true allyship. And that includes showing respect to event organizers and attendees.

It also includes designing presentations that go beyond snapshots of smiling white dudes.

Creating inclusive slide decks

After the publication of my first book, my coauthor Poornima and I created a presentation to share its key messages and drive awareness (and hopefully sales). After we outlined our talk, I dove into designing a slide deck, using stock photography and other images to reinforce our speaking points. And I purposefully chose images of women, taking the opportunity to showcase diversity — or so I thought.

I believed I'd done a good job with our slides, until we delivered that talk at the Palo Alto Lean In Circle meeting in January 2016. My daughter Emma, who was in the audience, gave me feedback afterward. She pointed out that all of the stock photography was of white women, most of whom had blond ponytails. Jeepers. I hadn't even noticed. (As you might have guessed, I immediately changed the slide deck to reflect more diversity.)

By contrast, I remember being happily surprised as I watched Joel Spolsky, CEO of Stack Overflow, deliver a keynote at Pluralsight LIVE a few years ago.[120] When he showed photos of software developers, they were all women of color.

Of course, the opportunity to showcase diversity is not limited to tech. In a talk for the Women in Medicine Summit 2020, Dr. Seth Trueger shared how he acts as an ally, including steering away from stock photos that pattern match a doctor as "a guy with white hair."

Think about the subtle — or not so subtle — messages you send wherever you use images. Not only in presentations and pitch decks, but also in your marketing collateral, in blog posts, and on your website. If you're showing only white, male, able-bodied people, what stereotypes are you reinforcing?

It may be understated, but the simple act of using stock photos and illustrations of people from underrepresented groups makes a difference. And there are many resources (some of which are free) to make it easy for you. I've listed several of my favorites in the "Additional Resources" section at the back of this book. You can also find them at *www.betterallies.com/resources*. Make them your go-to websites for finding stock images whenever you need to show a photo of a professional person.

Speaking is power

Public speaking and panel participation are activities typically reserved for powerful, talented, accomplished people with important ideas. When exclusively white people, men, or white men perform those activities, the underlying message is that those people — and only those people — are worthy. Allies know and celebrate the fact that many nonwhite, nonmale people are powerful, talented, and accomplished. When called on to speak, allies use their privilege to ensure that more voices have a turn at the mic.

Actions for Better Allies:
Share Speaking Opportunities

Allies who are truly dedicated to amplifying marginalized voices must be willing to give up a few choice speaking gigs so others may share their knowledge.

- If you're a man and are asked to speak as part of an all-male lineup, push back and/or decline.
- If you're white, say no to all-white panels.
- When you do present, ensure that your slide images show people from a variety of backgrounds, gender identities, body types, and abilities.
- If you're offered a speaking engagement but know someone from an underrepresented group who could do the job, connect them to the event organizer and pass on the spot yourself.

10

HIRING PRACTICES

The hiring pipeline is an easy scapegoat for why a workforce lacks diversity. You've probably heard the excuses. Maybe you've even made some of them yourself. I know I have.

- "There aren't enough women candidates."
- "We don't get many Black people applying for jobs."
- "We'd hire them if we could find them."
- "We post a job, and only men apply."

The list goes on.

Yet people who are members of these underrepresented groups are often bewildered. Many eager and qualified candidates, working hard to get hired, are passed over. They feel unnoticed. Invisible, even.

The tech industry, in particular, has a quantifiable problem compared to other industries that employ software engineers. For instance, roughly one-third of software engineers employed in health care, government, education, and nonprofits were women, compared to a dinky one-fifth in tech itself.[121]

Some might say there's "a higher bar" in tech than in other industries, and that tech companies don't want to "lower the bar" to hire members of underrepresented groups. This is just another excuse, and a bigoted one at that. Joelle Emerson, founder of diversity and inclusion consultancy organization Paradigm, writes:

> The concern about "lowering the bar" stems from an incorrect (and biased) belief that a company has a high bar designed to hire the best people, and the reason it hasn't hired more diverse people is that they aren't able to meet that bar. In fact, in many cases it's the opposite: companies have a poorly designed hiring bar that fails to adequately evaluate highly qualified, and often diverse, candidates.[122]

I've experienced this poorly designed hiring bar firsthand. Early in my career, I interviewed for a software engineering job on the same day and at the same company as my partner Tim. At that point, our resumes were almost identical. We'd graduated with computer science degrees from the same university. When we first entered the workforce, we'd worked at a research institute on the same project. We'd even published a technical paper together.

When Tim and I decided to move to Silicon Valley, we applied for jobs at many of the same companies, which was not surprising, given our common interests and experience.

What *was* surprising was what happened during one long day of interviews.

A large tech company brought us on-site to interview for software development roles. In side-by-side conference rooms, my partner and I talked with each person on the interview team. After someone interviewed Tim, they came to interview me, and vice versa. It went on for hours. In our rental car, on the way back to our hotel, we compared notes. And that's when I discovered the unconscious bias that had been in play.

As Tim shared the tough questions he'd been asked, I was shocked. By contrast, my interviews were superficial and skirted any difficult technical topics. I couldn't believe the difference. In the few seconds it took the interviewers to close the door to the room my husband was in, walk a handful of steps, and open the door to the room I was in, they lowered the bar. And they did so before I'd said a word on my own behalf.

Turns out, we both got job offers from that company. But there was no way I was joining a team that viewed me as a woman who lacked the same technical chops as a man. I declined, and I never looked back. I joined a different company and went on to build my career at places that valued my skills and talents regardless of my gender.

In addition to lowering the bar, companies find other ways to bungle the hiring process. Makinde Adeagbo, a software engineer who has worked at Pinterest, Dropbox, and Facebook, shared this story of an appalling interview experience he had to endure:

> The technical founder/CEO walked into the room to ask a few technical questions. He was the author of a large, open source project. So, while I'd never met him before, I recognized his name and expected a challenging interview. Shockingly, his first question had nothing to do with technology. "Why do all the Black kids sit at the same table at school?" he asked. I was taken aback but tried to explain the social dynamics that might be at play. He followed with, "Why is it no longer okay to say n****r?" [I'd] never had that cutting word said to me and had a serious choice to make. Should I stand up and leave, or treat this as a teaching moment? It took mettle, but I chose the latter and gave the best 3 minute summary of 20th-century race relations that I could come up with. I finished the interview loop and went back to campus. When the recruiter called and congratulated me on getting an offer, I immediately declined, citing "severe cultural differences." [123]

The rest of this chapter explores ideas for treating candidates equitably and strategies for hiring a more diverse workforce. Specifically, I'll share approaches I've used in consulting projects for companies who want to attract and hire underrepresented candidates. For these projects, I often use this checklist from the National Center for Women in Information Technology, slightly modified to include other underrepresented groups and non-tech fields:[124]

- Do you use language and images to convey that people from marginalized groups belong at your workplace?
- Do you emphasize an inclusive work culture?
- Do you showcase how your company's work is contributing to social good? The social value of work can attract candidates from marginalized groups.

While most clients I've worked with tend to do well in these three areas, there is always something for them to improve. And some of those areas for improvement are more surprising than others.

Creating a great careers web page

A company's careers page is one of the first places a potential employee will visit to learn more about the company's culture, working environment, and advancement opportunities. If your company is serious about attracting a diverse pool of candidates, make sure this page is welcoming to them.

Use diverse images and inclusive language

First, look at the photos on your company's careers page. Do the photos show people of all kinds thriving at the company? Or are they full of young white dudes having a good time? Here are some issues that I've flagged for past clients:

- A photo of a dozen people dressed in camouflage overalls and carrying paintball rifles. Ten men and one woman were standing and smiling. Another woman was sitting on the ground, not looking happy at all.

- A photo of employees enjoying a dance party, in what looked like a mosh pit. One man was on his back, held up by the others who jostled him around the pit. The red flag? As a woman, I couldn't imagine having others' hands all over my body, potentially even groping me. If this was how the company had fun, count me out.

- One company had a nice rotation of photos showing employees in different settings, yet the website always displayed the same one first: two white male cyclists wearing jerseys with the company logo. Why not lead with a photo showing more diversity?

Before you decide your own page is perfectly fine, put yourself in the shoes of an applicant from an underrepresented group. Imagine how a woman, a person of color, an older worker, a person with a disability, or a single parent would feel seeing the images on your careers page. Would they see people who look nothing like them, engaging in activities that broadcast an uninviting culture? Or would they see people from a variety of backgrounds in settings that showcase their enjoyment at work and value to the company? Candidates need to be able to envision themselves working somewhere, and seeing their own experience reflected through photos is a crucial way to do that. (I touched on this practice in Chapter 5 because the imagery used to promote events also needs to be diverse and inclusive.)

That said, be genuine and authentic. Use photos of your employees in a way that represents your demographics. In other words, don't try to deceive candidates by showcasing more diversity than you actually have. If you have only one (or a small number of people) of a given demographic, don't feature them as though they were the norm.

To be fully transparent, consider putting your diversity statistics on your careers page, along with an explanation of what you're doing to improve them. Do this not just for the overall employee population, but realize that many candidates will also look for diversity on your company's leadership page. If your executive team is mostly male and pale, explain any goals you have for improving representation there too.

Wondering what to do if you don't have a diverse workforce at all?

First up, don't use stock photography. It may be a tempting solution, but candidates can easily do an image search online and find that your "employee" is a model who appears on many job sites. (Yes, this happens. In doing research for this book, I quickly spotted a stock photo of a Black male model featured as though he were an employee on a Fortune 500 company's careers page.[125])

Secondly, you're going to have to emphasize how welcoming and inclusive you are through text, not photos. I'll explore this in the next section.

One last thing about photos. Keep in mind that candidates may use assistive technology such as screen readers. To help them understand what your images depict, be sure to add descriptions with HTML alt tags or in captions underneath the photos.

While photos are important, don't forget about the power of language in making people feel like they belong ... or not.

In describing their organizational culture, one of my clients, a small startup, emphasized the importance of their after-hour LAN parties. I have to admit I didn't know what a LAN party was, so I searched online and discovered that it's when a local area network (LAN) is used to connect people playing multiplayer video games. At the time, the Entertainment Software Association reported that about half of all computer/video gamers were women, but this ratio dropped to around 15 percent with massive multiplayer games.[126] This company might have been unintentionally eliminating women candidates by nurturing this aspect of their culture and emphasizing it on their careers page.

Zapier, a web app automation company, does so with the following statement:

> We're dedicated to building a warm, open, and inclusive work environment — one that's safe for people of all backgrounds. To this end, when you join our team, you agree to a code of conduct. And our steps to improve diversity and inclusion at Zapier are published in a public changelog.[127]

Another way to show a commitment to an inclusive culture is by offering resource or affinity groups for underrepresented employees. If these exist at your organization, be loud and proud about them on your careers page. For example, here's how the Massachusetts Institute of Technology (MIT) describes their groups:

> Employee Resource Groups (ERGs) are employee-led groups formed around common interests, issues and/or a common bond or background.
>
> ERG members create a positive work environment at MIT by actively contributing to the Institute's mission, values and efforts specific to inclusion, such as recruitment and retention. All of MIT's ERGs are open to any employee.
>
> MIT is pleased to support the following Employee Resource Groups.
> - African, Black, American, Caribbean (ABAC) ERG
> - Asian Pacific American (APA) ERG
> - Disabilities ERG
> - Latino ERG

- Lesbian, Bisexual, Gay, Transgender Queer (LBGTQ) ERG
- Millennials ERG
- Women in Technology (WIT) ERG[128]

Welcoming all candidates

Think about how you describe the kind of candidates you're looking for. Are you being welcoming to people from diverse backgrounds, ethnicities, sexual orientations, ages, and abilities? I especially appreciate the inclusive way Change.org does this:

> Your coworkers are high-impact, low-ego, and have a deep respect for our members. We expect you to be the same.
>
> All qualified applicants will receive consideration for employment without regard to race, colour, national origin, religion, sexual orientation, gender, gender identity, age, physical disability, or length of time spent unemployed.[129]

Did you notice that last phrase? "Length of time spent unemployed." This company encourages job seekers to apply even with resume gaps. Here's why I like that a lot.

Between 2008 and 2013, one in four Americans in their fifties lost their jobs. Many gave up looking after that economic downturn because they assumed a lapse in employment would be held against them.

More recently, we've seen the devastating impact of the COVID-19 pandemic on employment. Workforce reductions were swift and severe, and Black women and Latinas were hit hardest by the crisis. Many people stopped looking for work. For example, during September 2020, 1.1 million Americans dropped out of the workforce, 80% of whom were women.[130]

To attract workers who may have been forced out of work during that time, as well as others who have taken a break in their career for health or caregiving reasons, make it clear that you won't hold it against them.

Veterans are another group that you may want to specifically welcome to apply to your openings. Waste management company Republic Services prominently displays a button labeled "Veterans" on their careers page. Clicking it leads to a page showcasing veterans who are their employees, along with this message:

Hiring our Heroes

Republic Services has built its success on 5 values including Respect, Responsibility, Reliability, Resourcefulness and a Relentless focus on taking care of our customers. We have found that these values align well with those who are transitioning from military service. We actively recruit and hire recently transitioned military as well as those long discharged from active duty. Republic Services has a proven track record of hiring and developing those who have served as we value the skills, experience and operational excellence you bring to our organization and your commitment to a better tomorrow.

Republic Services provides training to help ensure a successful transition from military service to a career at Republic Services, and our culture of success through engaged, diverse teams helps all military veterans succeed in a variety of positions, including operations managers, maintenance technicians, drivers, and sales representatives.[131]

Here's one more idea for being inclusive on your careers page. (I've saved the best for last.) Encourage candidates to apply even if they don't meet all the requirements.

You've probably heard about a now-famous internal Hewlett-Packard study that found that women applied for a promotion only when they believed they met 100 percent of the qualifications listed for the job, while men applied when they thought they could meet 60 percent of the job requirements.[132]

Hewlett-Packard's findings have been validated by other research. In *How to Lead*, Jo Owen describes how men applied for head teaching roles when they thought they were 50 percent ready, while women wanted to be nearer to 100 percent ready before taking on the responsibility.[133] Leadership development trainer Tara Mohr dug deeper and found that the problem isn't a lack of confidence in women applicants. She polled more than a thousand men and women and found that both genders were likely to avoid applying for jobs if they believed they didn't meet the qualifications. In an article for the *Harvard Business Review*, Mohr writes:

> They didn't see the hiring process as one where advocacy, relationships, or a creative approach to framing one's expertise could overcome not having the skills and experiences outlined in the job qualifications. What held them back from applying was not a mistaken perception about themselves, but a mistaken perception about the hiring process.[134]

Want to attract more candidates for your open roles, especially for those that are hard to fill? Step one: Simplify your job descriptions, removing "preferred" skill sets and other requirements that aren't truly required. Step two: Consider adding this one sentence to your job ads, like website tool company Webflow:

> We'd love to hear from you — even if you don't meet 100% of the requirements.[135]

If your company contributes to social good, say so

As the National Center for Women in Information Technology points out, the social value of work can attract candidates from marginalized groups. If your company is mission-led, with a goal of being economically successful while also having a positive impact on society, be sure this is emphasized on the careers page.

Alternatively, if your company doesn't have such a mission, look for ways to appeal to candidates who want to contribute to social good. Does your organization offer volunteering opportunities? Do you have customers who utilize your product offerings for their own mission-driven strategic goals? I remember speaking with a company that launches satellites to collect data from space. As I asked about their customers, I heard inspiring stories. One utilized weather data to improve farming yields. Another relied on maritime traffic data to go after pirates. I encouraged them to showcase these stories on their careers page to share how they help customers make a positive impact in the world.

Emphasize employee benefits

Last but not least, review the language used to describe employee benefits on your company's careers page. While I recommend you have a link to a complete description of your benefits, highlight those that are particularly important to members of underrepresented groups. Here are some examples:

Benefits to Highlight

Parental leave (and not just for the person who gave birth)

Adoption assistance

On-site childcare

Eldercare

Domestic partner benefits

Trans-inclusive healthcare

Reproductive health coverage

Mentorship and sponsorship programs

While applicable to all, these benefits are especially important to women, who are the primary caregivers in our society.[136]

Whether through photos, the language used to describe your company's culture and social impact, employee benefits, or other means, members of marginalized groups will evaluate your company by your careers page. Think about the messages you want to send, and ensure that your website reinforces them.

Understanding bias in interviews

Bias can too easily creep into the interview process, like it did on that day my partner and I interviewed at the same company. And research shows the impact of bias. Resumes with African American–sounding names receive 50 percent fewer callbacks than resumes with white-sounding names. Candidates with accents, women, and working mothers are all rated less favorably than their peers.[137] Naturally, these biases lead to fewer hires of members of marginalized groups.

Then there's culture fit, and the age-old interview debrief question of, "Would you want to grab a beer with them?"

Back in the 1980s, culture fit and "chemistry" were all the rage. They sprang from the idea that if companies hired employees whose personalities and values aligned with organizational strategy, those employees would feel more invested in their jobs and become more loyal. Skills were important, but cultivating a workforce of like-minded people ran a close second. Over time, however, "culture fit" became code for something else: passing the friendship test. The whole "grab a beer" scenario prompted decision makers to begin thinking of "culture fit" as relating to likeability, personal similarities, and chemistry with the interviewer. It gave them license to hire people they wanted to hang out with, and pass over people who might've been ideal for the job but clashed with their leadership styles.[138]

Patty McCord, a human resources consultant and former chief talent officer at Netflix, points out the following about hiring for culture fit:

> You end up with this big, homogenous culture where everybody looks alike, everybody thinks alike, and everybody likes drinking beer at 3 o'clock in the afternoon with the bros.[139]

Fortunately, things are changing.

I remember attending a panel where Jeffrey Siminoff, who was then head of diversity at Twitter, made a truly memorable comment. "If I hear that a candidate isn't a culture fit, I ask if they could be a culture add." Right on.

In a similar vein, Aubrey Blanche, director of equitable design and impact at Culture Amp, recommends asking, "What will this candidate bring that we don't currently have on the team?"[140] Previously, Blanche worked at Atlassian, where they shifted their hiring focus from "culture fit" to "values fit." It helped recruiters hire people who shared the company's goals, but not necessarily the viewpoints or backgrounds of the interview team.[141]

Prove it again bias

Another kind of bias that can show up in the interview process is "prove it again" bias. Groups that have been stereotyped as less competent or hardworking often have to provide a larger, more compelling body of evidence to be judged as equally competent. Groups that have to "prove it again" include women, Black and Latinx people, individuals with disabilities, and Asian Americans.[142]

During the hiring process, this bias may mean that men who apply for managerial positions are evaluated based on their leadership potential, whereas women are judged on their past performance.[143] What does this look like in practice? "Before I'd hire her to lead a business unit, I'd want to make sure she's already been successful in that kind of role." For an equally qualified man, the comment might be: "Even though he hasn't led a business unit before, I just know he can do the job. He looks great."

Combating bias during the interview process

Soon after the COVID-19 crisis struck, I attended a "What's Next for Inclusive Hiring" webinar held by Joelle Emerson, CEO of Paradigm, a diversity and inclusion consulting firm.

During the webinar, we brainstormed ways that bias can creep into the virtual interviews that are now commonplace. For example, interviewers can get a peek into a candidate's life, which often reveals clues about their socio-economic or caregiving status. Do they have strong bandwidth? Do they have a laptop for the video meetings, or do they need to use the camera on their phone? What is the room like in the background? Are small children present?

To help reduce bias, one of the attendees said they updated their interview prep email to recommend that candidates find a plain background for interviews. What a simple idea, and a great way to support interviewees.

To take it to the next level, offer to reimburse candidates for childcare or adult care, rental costs for a laptop, and costs to travel to and use a meeting room in a coworking space. In fact, tech company GitLab provides this kind of financial support to any candidate who needs it.[144]

Here are some other ways to combat bias, including tactics for circumventing the "culture fit" trap:

- **Create objective criteria for reviewing resumes.**
  Choose the most critical requirements from the job description, and evaluate candidates on those qualities,

not on their gender, age, favorite song, or other qualities that don't equate to being able to do the work.

- **Redact unnecessary personal information.** Resumes can include information that you don't need to evaluate and that might create bias, such as a candidate's name, schools attended, and home address. Think about what you can strip from resumes or applications to reveal only what matters to your role.[145]

- **Use structured interview tactics.** Create interview questions focused on the skills and abilities your company is seeking. Ask each interviewee the same questions in the same order. (Don't make the same mistake as the team who interviewed my partner and me on the same day.)

- **Share interview questions ahead of time.** Set up candidates for success by telling them the questions to expect. This approach helps minimize performance anxiety, which may especially impact certain groups, including women.[146]

- **Create a standardized rubric for evaluating candidates.** Then rank every person on the same scale to help with decision making and eliminating "gut" feelings.[147]

- **Consider asking candidates to perform a work test.** Assign them a task that's similar to what they'd do if hired. Work tests are among the most reliable predictors of how someone will do in a job.[148]

- **Remind the interview team that bias can creep in.** Here's an approach that Google followed for removing bias from performance calibration sessions. In *Work Rules!*, Laszlo Bock describes how at the start of Google's calibration meetings, everyone is given a simple handout describing common errors and biases that assessors make and how to fix them.[149] Simply reminding managers of these biases was enough to eliminate many of them, and Google applied the same approach to interview teams. You can find their "unbiasing hiring" checklist online on their re:Work website.[150]

- **Restate the role and the experience you're looking for.** When the interview team meets to discuss candidates, get everyone on the same page. Remind them of the job requirements. You want to focus on the role and the candidate's experience, and avoid off-topic discussions of what someone liked or didn't like about a candidate, which might be based on bias.

- **Watch out for biased comments.** Here are some all-too-common phrases that should raise red flags during interview debriefs. (You saw some of them in Chapter 3.)

All-Too-Common Biased Comments

The candidate doesn't have that qualification (when discussing something not on the job description but that more privileged candidates meet).

They wouldn't want this role because of the travel.

Before hiring them, I'd like to see them prove they're capable (when discussing some responsibility that they've done in a previous job).

I don't want to lower the bar.

I'm not racist/sexist/homophobic, but ...

They wouldn't be a culture fit.

It's impossible to completely eliminate personal bias, but it's imperative to eliminate as much of it as possible. Especially for those who are truly committed to hiring workers from marginalized groups.

Want to better recognize your personal bias? Take a free, online implicit association test on Harvard's Project Implicit website.[151]

Evaluate potential new hires on their inclusion experience

If you're trying to build a more inclusive environment, "it makes sense to stop letting in folks who would work against that goal," says diversity and inclusion consultant Jason Wong.[152] This means screening for inclusive attitudes and experiences during the interview process.

One simple way to do this is to ask candidates a question or two about their inclusion experience. Here are a few suggestions:

Inclusion Experience Interview Questions

How have you contributed to an inclusive workplace culture or community?

Tell me about your experience working with diverse teams.

What have you done to ensure that coworkers feel a sense of belonging?

Have you had the opportunity to act as someone's ally at work? Tell me about it.

If you were to take steps to diversify your team, what would you *not* do?

By opening the door to this topic during the interview, I bet you'll be able to spot people who both talk the talk and walk the walk.

Pay attention to your interview team

When possible, make sure candidates meet at least one interviewer of their same gender, ethnicity, or age. By seeing someone "like them," candidates from underrepresented groups may feel more at ease and do better in the interview process. At Cisco, this practice resulted in a roughly 50 percent increase in the odds that a woman would be hired for a given position.[153]

That said, you don't want to burden employees from underrepresented demographics by asking them to do more interviewing than their peers. Being on an interview panel takes time away from the work that is going to be measured as part of quarterly or annual assessments. If you are tasking certain people with more than their fair share of interviewing, what can you do to reward them or set them up for success with the rest of their job responsibilities?

Lastly, make sure that all members of your interview panel have a real and respected voice in evaluating candidates. If you're inviting someone to be on your panel so that candidates can meet with someone "like them," their perspective should matter just as much as the rest of the panel.

Find the leaks

If it looks like your company is not netting enough applicants from underrepresented groups, find out why. Evaluate your process, identify where these candidates drop out, and iterate. Use metrics from HR or your recruiting team to understand where candidates from underrepresented backgrounds drop out during the hiring process. Is it during phone screens? Interviews? After the offer is made? Find out what's going wrong at which phase, and change that step.

One last thing

As you onboard new hires from underrepresented groups, consider that they might feel tokenized. They might believe that you hired them solely because you wanted a more diverse workforce, not because they were perfectly suited to the position. They might also be concerned that their new coworkers think the bar was lowered to make them an offer. They might hear someone say, "You're a diversity hire."

Here's a fantastic idea that Larissa Shapiro, a diversity and inclusion leader, shared with me:

> Over our latest cohorts of interns, we have succeeded in massively changing the gender and ethnic diversity. And the students did seem to wonder if we had chosen them for their demographics, not their skills. I walked them through how we screen for interns, explaining how you only get through the (very) large initial pool by scoring well on our anonymized online code assessment, and that therefore the bar is no different for any of them. I explained how bias traditionally skews the selection process and how by blocking bias, we get the best talent, which is them. I could see the women and PoC [people of color] interns relax when we got through this. The screening is a firm and anonymized bar, and that helps.[154]

Similarly, after software company Clio introduced a goal to hire more women, they made sure that every manager took the time to explain to new employees (regardless of gender) why they were hired and why Clio was excited they chose to accept their offer. They also made sure each woman who joined understood the company goal and how it worked, "instead of maybe hearing about it around the proverbial water cooler and creating her own narrative about it."[155]

Before wrapping up this section, I have one more tip: When hiring or promoting someone, be clear it's because they're the best person for the job. As Franklin Leonard, founder of The Black List, points out in a series of tweets:[156] [157]

Franklin Leonard ✓ @franklinleonard · Nov 22, 2019   ○○○
Don't tell people you hired or promoted someone because of their
"diverse perspective."

If that's part of it, then they got the job because they have a better
understanding of your audience than the other candidates, which means
they were the best candidate.

Say that.

　○ 6　　　　　　 ⇅ 136　　　　　　 ♡ 944　　　　　　 ⬆

Franklin Leonard ✓ @franklinleonard · Nov 22, 2019   ○○○
Saying you hired someone because of their "diverse perspective" is
simply code for "I'm a good person because I hired someone that doesn't
look like me" and simultaneously undervalues all the other contributions
that person will make.

　○ 2　　　　　　 ⇅ 10　　　　　　 ♡ 142　　　　　　 ⬆

In other words, take the opportunity to set them up for success.

This chapter offers some key insights on the topic of allyship in hiring practices, but there's so much more to learn. In fact, I wrote *The Better Allies Approach to Hiring* so I could dig deeper into equitable hiring practices. To learn more — including guidelines for writing inclusive job descriptions and attracting a diverse candidate pool — I hope you'll consider checking out this companion guidebook.

Actions for Better Allies:
Strive to Hire Equitably

Allies can band together to banish the "leaky pipeline" excuses and focus on employing strategies that are proven to attract and hire applicants from underrepresented groups. Here are some ways you can make this possible in your organization:

- Ensure that your company's careers web page uses language and images to convey that people from marginalized groups are welcome and belong in your workplace.
- Create interview processes and teams that will set up candidates for success, and prep interviewers to be aware of hidden biases.
- Implement structured interviews for open positions.
- Evaluate candidates on their inclusion experience, using the suggested questions in this chapter.
- Emphasize that employees were hired because they were highly qualified, to combat any concern that they're just a "diversity hire."

GIVING FEEDBACK

Wondering why we don't have more women in leadership roles across corporate America? Researchers at Stanford University's Clayman Institute can point to one of the reasons: the vague feedback that women tend to receive over their careers.

By analyzing performance reviews from three large tech companies and a professional services company, the researchers at Clayman uncovered some telling differences in the kind of feedback given to men versus women. They found that women were less likely than men to receive specific feedback tied to outcomes. This was true for both praise and constructive feedback. By contrast, men were offered a clearer picture of what they were doing well, how their performance was impacting the business, and what they needed to do to get promoted.[158]

The study also found other gendered differences in the performance reviews, specifically in the language used. When women were praised, they were twice as likely to receive feedback on team contributions versus individual accomplishments, which could hold them back during performance calibration and promotion discussions. Women were also described as "supportive," "collaborative," and "helpful" twice as often as men, and, interestingly, received 76 percent of the references of being "too aggressive." Men's reviews included words like "drive," "transform," "innovate," and "tackle" twice as often as women. Let's face it: The language used to describe men represents highly valued traits in many industries. The language used to describe women, on the other hand, is subjective and difficult to interpret.

I've seen some of this firsthand. A few years back, a tech company asked me to lead a career development workshop for a group of women employees. Beforehand, I was given access to their profiles and the kudos they'd received. One woman caught my eye because of two vastly different endorsements she received for the same project:

> A big thanks to Sue for spearheading improvements to our product support portal. Very quick on the uptake and always responsive!

> Congratulations, Sue, on your two-year anniversary at our company! You've done outstanding things in your first two years, including rebuilding the product support portal to scale with our $100M enterprise business.

As I read the first one, I felt it was superficial and rushed. The reviewer didn't identify how being "quick on the uptake" led to having an impact on customer satisfaction or bottom-line results. By contrast, the second reviewer clearly recognized Sue's impact: that she had rebuilt a key product, allowing the business to scale to $100 million.

The Stanford study isn't the only one to report disparities in how men and women receive professional feedback. Kieran Snyder, cofounder and CEO of Textio, applied linguistic analysis to performance reviews. She collected and analyzed 248 reviews from 180 people, including 105 men and 75 women from 28 different companies, in her study. Interestingly, 59 percent of the reviews received by men and 88 percent of those received by women contained critical feedback. And the suggestions given to women for improvement were more likely to focus on emotions, personality, and tone. Those given to men were more concrete, direct, and actionable.[159]

Finally, a 2020 Lean In report titled "The State of Black Women in Corporate America" points out that Black women typically receive less support from their managers than white coworkers. For example, only 36 percent of Black women surveyed agreed that "My manager provides opportunities for me to showcase my work," compared to 39 percent of white women and 43 percent of white men.[160]

Dr. Shelley Correll and Dr. Caroline Simard of the Clayman Institute point out:

> Clearly, these dynamics can disadvantage women at promotion time. Without specific, documented business accomplishments, it is difficult for a manager to make the case for advancement. Conversely, if a business objective was missed, a lack of frank feedback deprives women of the opportunity to hit the mark next time.[161]

Of course, managers have to know about the larger business unit or corporate strategy in order to tie performance feedback to business outcomes. Unfortunately, not all managers do.

A few years ago, I was coaching a group of women at a large tech company, leading a discussion on the importance of talking about the impact of our work. Many people, especially those who are early in their careers, tend to identify a long list of accomplishments when writing annual self-appraisals or updating their resumes. A better approach, as pointed out in the Clayman research, is to tie work to the business outcome by describing the impact of all these tasks. For example, instead of "fixed 40 bugs," an engineer might write, "fixed all bugs blocking renewal sales of

$5M." For the women I was coaching that day, this approach was novel — and, frankly, hard. Many didn't know why their manager prioritized certain tasks over others; many didn't know the higher-level goals of their division. So I encouraged them to ask their managers before our next meeting.

When we spoke again a month later, four of the fifteen women shared some striking news. Their managers were not able to answer questions about the business impact of their projects. And get this: Because those women didn't want to handicap their career growth, they immediately applied for an internal transfer. They wanted to work for managers who could be better allies by talking about the impact of their work and giving them feedback about how to have an even bigger impact.

How race and identity affect professional feedback

Gender bias is becoming more widely documented, but women are not the only group to receive mixed or misleading professional feedback. Within Black communities, it's common for people to coach each other on the fact that they need to be "twice as good" as their white counterparts to achieve the same levels of success, and research shows that this is not far off. According to a study by Costas Cavounidis and Kevin Lang of Boston University, Black workers receive extra scrutiny from their supervisors, which can lead to less favorable or constructive performance reviews, lower wages, and even job loss. With increased surveillance comes increased employee nervousness. Small mistakes are more likely to be caught, which, over time leads to negative feedback and reduced pay. This research demonstrates how discrimination factors into company decisions, creating a feedback loop that results in ever-increasing racial gaps in the labor force.[162]

Gender identity and sexual orientation also affect workplace feedback. In a survey of LGBTQ Americans conducted by Harvard's T.H. Chan School of Public Health, 22 percent reported that they were not paid equally or promoted at the same rate as their straight and cisgender peers.[163] According to a nationally representative survey of transgender people in the United States by the National Center for Transgender Equality, 27 percent of respondents said they had experienced being not hired, fired, or not promoted due to their gender identity or expression.[164] And an in-depth report on the financial penalty for LGBT women in America — co-authored in 2020 by the Center for American Progress and the Movement Advancement Project — stated that for every dollar a man in a married-opposite-sex couple earns, a woman in a same-sex couple earns $0.79 whereas a man in a same-sex couple earns $0.98.[165] Clearly, this lack of actionable feedback is impacting earning potential.

The bottom line? When unconscious bias plays into performance appraisals and feedback, it can lead to inaccuracy and unfair treatment based on age, gender, race, ability, religion, appearance, sexual orientation, and other traits. Members of all underrepresented groups may struggle to obtain constructive, actionable feedback. And this means they will have a harder time improving their performance and advancing in their careers, keeping them from moving into visible roles and leadership positions. Without quality feedback, members of marginalized groups have a difficult time penetrating the upper echelons of workplace power.

Undoing bias about who "looks like a leader"

A U.S. Naval Academy study of performance reviews for more than four thousand leaders found that supervisors often assume women in leadership roles have communal qualities (e.g., being nurturing, relationship-focused, and collaborative), and that these are perceived to be less valuable than agentic characteristics (e.g., being instrumental, task-focused, and goal-oriented), which male leaders are assumed to possess. As a result, women don't "look like leaders" and get penalized for that. In an article for *Behavioral Scientist*, the study's authors revealed the following insights:

> Our findings suggest that people from underrepresented groups can be penalized for not looking like a leader, and are told implicitly that they are not leaders through the messaging of performance evaluations.
>
> As a result, women in leadership positions face an impossible situation. They will either receive feedback highlighting their lack of feminine, communal attributes ("She's not compassionate or organized enough"), criticizing them for taking too much power ("She's abrasive, overbearing"), or for lacking some key leadership qualification ("She's inept, temperamental"). No matter their leadership style, they are deemed unfit.[166]

This particular study focused on a military academy and was performed by Naval Academy researchers, but their conclusions are supported by findings in the corporate world. Business consultancy Gartner has reported that qualified candidates from underrepresented groups are not getting due consideration for leadership roles because of both unconscious and conscious bias in hiring and promotion decisions.[167] So many private companies pay lip service to the idea of a diverse workforce, yet hesitate to elevate people from underrepresented groups to management, leadership, or C-level positions. A lack of constructive feedback exacerbates the situation.

One piece of advice from the authors of the Naval Academy study? (Spoiler alert: You've heard this one already.) Be specific and clear about evaluation criteria. Doing so helps reduce bias and stereotyping based on personality traits.[168]

Avoiding gatekeeping

When she was an undergraduate mathematics/economics major, Anna Gifty tweeted that a professor tried to discourage her from pursuing a PhD in economics:[169]

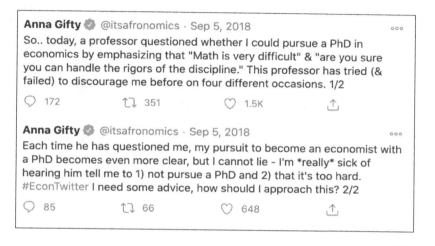

Anna Gifty ✔ @itsafronomics · Sep 5, 2018

So.. today, a professor questioned whether I could pursue a PhD in economics by emphasizing that "Math is very difficult" & "are you sure you can handle the rigors of the discipline." This professor has tried (& failed) to discourage me before on four different occasions. 1/2

💬 172   🔁 351   ♡ 1.5K   ⬆

Anna Gifty ✔ @itsafronomics · Sep 5, 2018

Each time he has questioned me, my pursuit to become an economist with a PhD becomes even more clear, but I cannot lie - I'm *really* sick of hearing him tell me to 1) not pursue a PhD and 2) that it's too hard. #EconTwitter I need some advice, how should I approach this? 2/2

💬 85   🔁 66   ♡ 648   ⬆

In sharp contrast, Dr. Patty Lopez responded with what she does in similar situations:[170]

Dr Patty Lopez @pittrpatt · Sep 7, 2018

When I see someone who I don't know at an event, I assume they belong and introduce myself. When someone asks me if they should try research, do something new, switch managers, change employers, I connect them to my network. #DontBeAGateKeeper @betterallies

Gatekeeping feedback is common and often slips out unconsciously. If you're in a position to give someone constructive comments, you may think you're doing so based solely on their performance or role, but your choice of words may betray unconscious bias. For instance, Harvard researchers examined teacher evaluations and found that men were more

often described as "brilliant" and "genius" or praised for their
innovative ideas, while women were more often acknowledged
for their kind demeanor and execution.[171]

One quick way to check feedback for gatekeeping bias: Ask
yourself, "Would I give the same feedback to someone of a
different identity or background?" Kristen Pressner, a global HR
executive, gave a TEDx talk on bias and recommended the "flip
it to test it" experiment, saying:

> Maybe you are a superhuman person who manages to
> intercept those brain shortcuts at exactly the right moment to
> ensure you're behaving bias-free and consistently with your
> values, and beliefs, and all of your actions. It could very well
> be. But what have you got to lose to double-check yourself? If
> we all started to flip it to test it, we might just be surprised at
> how often we would choose to behave differently. Because
> what if you're missing an opportunity to see the world
> differently?[172]

Paying attention to pay

Did you know that women and employees of color receive less
compensation than white men even when they receive equal
scores on performance evaluations?[173] I wish I had known this
back when I was an executive leading large software engineering
teams. While I like to think that I awarded increases equitably,
regardless of race and gender, this statistic makes me wonder.

I also wonder if there might have been a larger issue of pay
inequity, based on employee's starting salaries or prior
performance evaluations, that I could've addressed.

The problem is that many organizations still feel comfortable
offering lower salaries to qualified women. You've probably
heard the stats about women earning less than their male
counterparts, and that women of color earn even less. And you

might have thought, "Okay, but that doesn't happen at my company." Well, are you sure? Here are just a few data points:

- Since 2000, U.S. income growth for Black workers has been slower than for white workers in every wage bracket.[174]
- Women of color working in full-time, year-round positions earn 63 percent of what white men earn, much less than the 79 percent that white women earn.[175]
- On average, Black men earn 87 cents for every dollar that a white man earned.
- On average, Latino men earn 91 cents for every dollar earned by white men.[176]
- Women software engineers receive 83 percent of the salary that male software engineers receive.[177]
- Women financial managers earn 71 percent of what their male counterparts earn.[178]
- Women EMTs and paramedics earn 66 percent of what men are paid.[179]

When Salesforce CEO Mark Benioff heard concerns in 2015 that his company was paying women less than men, he was initially in denial. Yet, a company audit uncovered a statistical difference in pay between genders. Benioff admitted, "It was everywhere. It was through the whole company, every department, every division, every geography."[180] Over the next two years, Salesforce spent almost $6 million to close the gap.

Many other companies have since followed Salesforce's lead, including my former employer Adobe. However, there is still work to do. Starting in April 2018, all companies that employ 250 or more people in the U.K. were legally required to reveal their gender pay gaps. And the reports weren't good. Many companies reported mean pay gaps of over 50 percent.[181]

Allies should also know that (in tech, at least) as women gain experience, their pay gap with men widens. Here's what this looks like: Within the first two years of working in tech, women ask for and receive 98 percent of what their male counterparts make. Then, with thirteen or fourteen years of experience, women ask for 94 cents for every dollar and *receive* just 92 cents for every dollar that men make.[182] Over time, the impact can be staggering.

For example, imagine two equally qualified, thirty-five-year-old software engineers, one a man and one a woman. Let's assume the man's annual salary is $150,000, and the woman earns 92 percent of that, or $138,000. That means the woman is earning $1000 less than the man every month. (Wow.) Now, assume they work for thirty more years, both receiving a three percent cost of living increase each year and no other raises. By the time they retire at age 65, the man will earn almost $30,000 more than the woman annually. Adding up the income difference each year over the thirty years, the man will have earned $600,000 more than the woman, not counting additional benefits that might be tied to base salary, such as bonuses or employee stock purchase programs.

While this widening gap issue may not hold true in all industries, women face pay-related obstacles no matter where they work. And their lifetime earning potential suffers. A multi-industry study shows that women ask for raises just as often as men, but are less likely to get them.[183]

If your company hasn't already instituted a pay equity review, you have work to do. Do you have the power to make this happen for your team — or, better yet, for your larger function or business unit? If so, use your privilege to move your organization toward pay equity. And just like when giving feedback, be sure to use objective criteria to help curb biases when evaluating requests for increased salary or responsibility.

Why feedback matters and how to do it right

In 2016, McKinsey and Lean In performed a survey and found that women are less likely than men to receive difficult feedback — almost 20 percent less likely.

More recently, Dr. Shelley Correll of Stanford University's Clayman Institute performed an analysis of more than 200 performance reviews inside a large tech company. She found that leaders often give male employees specific (and sometimes harsh) feedback that helps them achieve specific goals, while women more commonly receive vague, personality-based feedback. Correll and her researchers also found that 60 percent of developmental feedback linked to business outcomes was given to men; only 40 percent was given to women.[184]

Why would this happen? Both studies cited a number of reasons, including:

- It can be difficult to give constructive feedback because we don't want to upset someone. And this is especially true for male managers giving feedback to women employees.

- It can also be uncomfortable to give feedback to someone who is different from us — not just another gender, but a different race, sexual orientation, or educational background. We might think, "If I point out how Aliyah, a graduate of a coding bootcamp, could have done a better job fixing that bug, she might think I'm biased against people who don't hold college degrees in computer science." To avoid this perception, we might soften the feedback.[185]

In *Radical Candor*, Kim Scott explores why it may be harder for men to be radically candid with women. She writes, "Most men are trained from birth to be 'gentler' with women than with men. Sometimes this can be very bad for the women who work for them."[186] In other words, men might hold back from criticizing women employees because they're afraid they might cry.

Scott reminds us that criticism is a gift and that it needs to be given out in equal measures to all employees. Sounds good, but how do we actually make it so? If your company isn't already offering training on how to give feedback equitably, ask about it.

Whether your company has such training or not, here are some suggestions from the Clayman Institute for how supervisors can be more effective in evaluating employees equitably and giving them feedback:

- Identify the criteria you'll use to evaluate employees at each level, and apply those criteria consistently.
- With each employee, discuss how their work has impacted the business.
- Tie all feedback, both positive and constructive, to business goals. For example, instead of just "Become a more strategic leader," you could say, "Become a more strategic leader by better understanding our competition and making recommendations to gain market share."
- Tell employees about the expertise you see them already exhibiting, and how they can develop more job-related skills.
- Write reviews of similar lengths so that you give roughly the same level of detailed feedback to all employees.[187]

Evaluating employees on inclusive behavior

As your company identifies objective criteria for evaluating employees, consider measuring how inclusive employees are. The more feedback people receive on inclusivity, the more it will become an ingrained behavior for them. In an article for the

Harvard Business Review, two human capital professionals at Deloitte Australia shared six traits or behaviors that distinguish inclusive leaders from others:

- **Visible commitment.** They articulate authentic commitment to diversity, challenge the status quo, hold others accountable, and make diversity and inclusion a personal priority.
- **Humility.** They are modest about capabilities, admit mistakes, and create the space for others to contribute.
- **Awareness of bias.** They show awareness of personal shortcomings as well as flaws in the system, and they work hard to ensure meritocracy.
- **Curiosity about others.** They demonstrate an open mindset and deep curiosity about others, listen without judgment, and seek with empathy to understand those around them.
- **Cultural intelligence.** They are attentive to others' cultures and adapt as required.
- **Effective collaboration.** They empower others, pay attention to diversity of thinking and psychological safety, and focus on team cohesion.[188]

One last thing

Feedback is a two-way street. Allies can check in with their team and let them know they're working to become a better ally for underrepresented groups. They can ask, "What's one thing I could be doing differently to better support you or to create a more inclusive workplace?" And then they can take action.

Actions for Better Allies:
Give Effective and Equitable Feedback

Feedback can be tricky to give, but it truly is a gift to receive. Without clear feedback, members of marginalized groups will have a much harder time succeeding and advancing. So, as an ally, remember:

- When giving feedback, focus on the business impact of an employee's work. What should they keep doing because it's moving the business forward? How should they improve in order to have an even bigger impact?
- Don't ease up just to avoid hurt feelings. Remember, vague feedback holds people back from growing in their careers.
- Tell them about the expertise you see in them and how to develop more job-related skills.
- Use objective criteria to evaluate employees in similar roles.
- Write reviews of roughly the same length for everyone on your staff.
- Ask for feedback on how you can be a better ally.

12

OPENING CAREER DOORS

During the late 1980s, my partner Tim and I both worked at an applied research center at Brown University. Because of the economic recession at the time, the center's funding from corporate partners started to dry up, and we knew we were facing a downsizing. So, we offered our resignations and decided to follow a dream we shared: to move to England, where Tim had spent his early childhood.

Soon after giving our notice to resign, my manager, Norm Meyrowitz, approached me with some exciting news. He had just met with two researchers who were visiting from a suburb of London, mentioned that I was moving there, and strongly recommended they hire me. (Knowing Norm, he probably told them they'd be stupid not to.) He could have been bitter about my resignation, but instead he opened a door for me, both literally and figuratively. He brought me into the conference room to meet them, and I joined their research group about two months later.

Fast forward five years, and Tim and I were living in the San Francisco Bay Area. I was working as a localization manager for Macromedia when I became pregnant with our first child. There came the morning when I looked in the mirror at my expanding waistline and realized it was time to tell my coworkers. Later that day, I had a one-on-one meeting with our vice president, Joe Dunn. He started by saying, "Karen, I have an opportunity to tell you about. I want you to run the quality engineering team for the company, and it comes with a promotion to the director level."

I didn't miss a beat, and responded, "That sounds great — and by the way, I'm pregnant, I want to take four months of maternity leave, and when I come back, I want to work part-time." I remember his response to this day. It was an enthusiastic, "*Cool!*" His support was outstanding.

And then there was the time I knew someone acting as my sponsor had opened the equivalent of double French doors for my career. Years had passed, I was now a vice president of engineering at Macromedia, and the company was being acquired by Adobe. I attended a meeting with several members of Adobe's leadership team, and during a break, one of them approached me and said, "Karen, I've really been looking forward to meeting you. Let's find time to talk soon about expanding your role and responsibilities once we complete the acquisition." Clearly, someone had been paying me some major compliments behind my back. It was sponsorship at its finest. I never discovered who my sponsor was, but I was so grateful they used their political clout to talk about me and open this major career door. I went on to work for that Adobe executive, with a much bigger role than I'd had before the acquisition.

These are just some examples of how allies have opened career doors over the course of my career. This type of support can take many shapes in addition to the ones I've described here. As I discussed in the previous chapter, giving the right kind of feedback can help someone grow their career. But it's also important to give stretch assignments and other learning opportunities, provide recommendations and referrals, and advocate effectively during performance calibration meetings and promotion discussions.

In an article titled "How to Be a Better Ally to Your Black Colleagues," Wharton professor Dr. Stephanie Creary shared a simple strategy for helping Black employees advance more quickly and gain career traction: Ask them about their work and their goals. Here's what she wrote:

> Inquiry can be a powerful tool to create connection when people can effectively read social situations and body language. However, when done without care — for example, by focusing on their racial backgrounds, personal lives, or their physical appearance — inquiry can feel overly invasive and harmful to Black workers. To improve the quality of your relationships with your Black colleagues, ask them about their actual work, including what they are hoping to accomplish, any concerns they have about doing that, and how you might be able to help them reach their vision.[189]

Career advancement support from allies can also take the form of seeing opportunities where others might see walls. Rachana Bhide, who we heard from earlier in the book, collects stories from women about their male allies. In her Corner of the Court Project, I read about Dr. Oksana Malysheva and Geoffrey Frost, a former CMO of Motorola. Malysheva wrote, "Three weeks after my daughter was born, I received a phone call from Geoffrey. He right away launched into the project he wanted me to lead, and the promotion that came with it. I was excited but honest with him about my need to be with my daughter." Pushing past the walls she was constructing in her mind, Frost focused on the flexibility and autonomy of the new role, and why it would be the perfect position for her as a new mother.[190]

Avoiding assumptions about career goals

I bet that Frost was familiar with Malysheva's career goals and identified that opportunity for her as a result. However, I've heard too many stories describing situations where this hasn't been the case. For example, one of my coaching clients was working on a fast-growing engineering team when the team's leader identified the need for a project manager to keep all their work on track. He asked my client, the only woman on the team, to take on this role. It might have been an awesome opportunity, except that it wasn't at all aligned with her career goal to become a software quality manager.

I heard from Jenny, a vice president of engineering, who, when her role was eliminated, received advice from her manager that she take an individual contributor role in the marketing department. It was a big step down in terms of responsibility and pay, and it felt like a slap in the face to her. Jenny's manager assumed she would take any job to stay on the payroll. Instead of helping her find a role, even externally, that would align with her goals and leverage her leadership experience, he nudged her toward voluntary demotion.

As my friend Julie Kratz, author of *Lead Like an Ally*, shared with me: "For allies, it's all about listening to what she wants and not advising her. I think men jump the gun often and want to 'save the day,' rather than create a win-win for both." Kratz then told me she had just spoken to a male ally that morning. He leads a large marketing team and recently reached out to high-potential women in the company about a new role on his team. All of them turned him down because they didn't want the travel that would come with the job. Kratz encouraged him to have a deeper conversation: Ask what they wanted to do in three years, discuss options for how he could be flexible regarding travel, and identify how this opportunity would be an ideal assignment to allow them to build skills needed to help them reach their career goals.

Because of ingrained workplace dynamics, it may be necessary for allies to do more than offer opportunities or ask general questions. Sometimes, allies need to help promising candidates from underrepresented groups articulate their goals by reflecting on their worries. Sometimes allies need to be sounding boards before they can become door openers.

The best stretch assignments are glamour work

Let's face it: Not all assignments are created equal. As Joan C. Williams and Marina Multhaup, researchers at the Center for WorkLife Law at the University of California, point out, "Some can set you up for promotion and skyrocket you to the top of your company — we call them glamour work. Other assignments are necessary but unsung. We call them office housework." And their research shows that women and people of color often wind up with worse assignments than their white male counterparts. Men get the glamour work while women and people of color get stuck with office housework. (Which, as we learned in Chapter 7, hinders their ability to be promoted.)[191]

What does glamour work look like in practice? More often than not, it's high profile. It might be developing an innovative product that is being sponsored by a senior vice president. It might be joining a task force to identify new revenue streams, giving a keynote on behalf of one's company, or doing groundbreaking research.

But it can also include lower-profile stretch assignments that provide the opportunity to learn new skills and achieve better positioning for a promotion. Such assignments can also help increase confidence, enhance social networks, and build credibility across an organization. As a result, stretch assignments can help retain employees from underrepresented groups. These challenging or prominent assignments may even keep them from dropping out of the field completely.[192]

Given all these benefits, allies should leverage glamour work to open career doors for marginalized colleagues. And if allies truly want to both cultivate and *retain* a diverse workforce, assigning these choice projects to people from underrepresented groups will further that goal. So why, as those researchers from the Center for WorkLife Law found, do men get a higher portion of glamour assignments?

Perhaps it comes down to our networks. If managers don't know marginalized colleagues and their career goals, how would they know to tap them for these career-building opportunities? (If this is the case for you, go back to Chapter 4 for actions to diversify your network.)

Or is it because it's convenient to hand off office housework to the people who first come to mind (often women and colleagues of color), thereby giving white men more time to build skills that will make them better candidates for glamour work? (Review Chapter 7 to avoid this tendency.)

Regardless of the reason, allies can turn this tide.

The next time you need someone to stand in for you on an initiative or take on a high-profile assignment, reflect on your selection criteria. Do you tend to give glamour work to certain people or certain types of people? What would it take to expand that pool? If you know only a few people who have the skills you value for these plum assignments, you might need to expand your network. Or figure out how more people, especially people outside your normal go-to list, can learn more of those skills.

My friend Jo Miller, CEO of Be Leaderly, offered the following advice for ensuring that stretch assignments and glamour work are distributed more equitably:

- Create a company-wide system for flagging available stretch assignments so they're offered in a way that's not political, biased, or promoting favoritism.
- Foster a failure-friendly environment where all employees aren't afraid to stretch, take risks, innovate, and learn.
- Provide employees with clear, frequent feedback — both formal and informal — so they can accurately gauge their readiness to take on stretch assignments.
- Encourage members of underrepresented groups to "round up" their assessment of their own skills as they evaluate their readiness for a stretch assignment or next-level job. (Turns out that men do this, while women tend to "round down" their skills.)[193]

While we're on the subject of talking about one's skills, Miller has some additional advice. In her book, *Woman of Influence: 9 Steps to Build Your Brand, Establish Your Legacy*, she explains how women can face a backlash when they advocate for themselves and talk about their achievements. It's because this behavior goes against cultural expectations for women. Yet, women need to talk about their accomplishments to be seen as being competent.

To combat this "damned if you do, doomed if you don't" conundrum, Miller recommends creating a culture where accomplishments are regularly recognized and celebrated. Doing so can normalize it for everyone. Consider adding "Humble Brags" as a regular agenda item during weekly meetings, creating a Slack channel for sharing wins, and so on.

Glamour work is desirable work, work that opens doors and ignites careers. It's essential for allies to find ways to spread that joy around.

The role mentors play

Here's a surefire way to make sure more people in your professional network have the skills to tackle glamour work: mentor them. Or ask someone who has the right skills to mentor them. And to be a better ally, focus on mentoring people from underrepresented groups.

Not only will mentees learn skills, they may also feel more engagement with your company, which will help them become more successful overall. As I learned from Brad Johnson and David Smith in their book *Athena Rising*, students at the Naval Academy rely on their upper-class mentors to pass along "the gouge" — salient tips for surviving, thriving, and avoiding big trouble. Mentors aren't just there to build confidence in their mentees; they can help prepare them for new challenges by sharing their own experiences and wisdom.

Which begs the question: Are members of underrepresented groups at your company receiving the equivalent of "the gouge"? Do they have access to mentors willing to give them the inside scoop?

If not, they may feel hamstrung. Six years after releasing their first diversity reports, Alphabet, Apple, Facebook, Microsoft, and Twitter have shown only low single-digit increases in their percentage of Black employees, according to CNBC.[194] While many factors contribute to these numbers, one of them could be that Black workers feel left out of "the know." They may never have been mentored on how to thrive or counseled on staying connected to key networking activities. They may not be in the loop on important discussions or have influential friends who can recommend their work.

One thing white allies can do to change this cultural tendency is mentor BIPOC at their companies. Is this you, but you're not sure where to start? If you have an employee group for Black or Latinx people, reach out to its leadership and ask for advice about your next steps. Do your part to ensure that all promising employees are in the know, regardless of background.

If mentorship feels like too much of a commitment right now, consider acts of micro-sponsorship instead. Lori Nishiura Mackenzie and Dr. Caroline Simard of Stanford's Clayman Institute compiled a list of ways to be a micro-sponsor to your colleagues from underrepresented groups. Many of these are phrased to apply to women colleagues, but the same strategies could be used for a coworker of color, a trans coworker, a disabled coworker, or anyone likely to benefit from acts of ally support:

- Affirm a person's competency. For example, acknowledge a woman leader's key contribution to her peers in a meeting or public forum.

- In team meetings, notice when women's contributions are overlooked. When someone else gets credit for her idea, add a comment such as "I'm glad you picked up on X's idea" to bring back the credit to her.

- In discussions of talent, ask clarifying questions when you suspect bias. Ask, for example, "What do we mean, exactly, when we say she is not strategic? How are we applying this criteria across all candidates?" or "You say she is aggressive, yet I don't see her exhibiting different communication behaviors than her colleagues."

- When you hear others discuss big assignments, bring up the names of top women talent as potential candidates.[195]

Here's another idea, especially if patents are important to your company's strategy.

Several years ago, *Fast Company* published a story that started with: "In today's installment of unsurprising-yet-still-depressing news: Women of color, particularly Black and Hispanic women, are less likely to obtain U.S. patent rights than white women and men."[196]

Allies can actively work to change this ratio by encouraging women of color to file patents for the work they're doing, and by mentoring them along the way. Or consider what a staff engineer at Intel did to scale her efforts beyond just one mentee. She started a quarterly workshop on the company's patent-filing process to demystify it for everyone, especially women.

Getting more women involved with patent work is not only good for their careers, it's also good for business. Research by the National Center for Women in Information Technology shows that mixed-gender teams produced the most frequently cited software patents — with citation rates 26 percent to 42 percent higher than the norm for similar patents.[197] What does this mean? Patent filings cite other patents to reference prior art that they've built on or to differentiate themselves. A patent that is cited frequently may be core to its field, meaning that it represents significant innovation. Simply stated, you're more likely to create a significant patent if you have a gender-diverse team.

Giving wholehearted recommendations

Recommendations come in many forms. Formal letters, social media endorsements, verbal reference checks, and back-channel casual conversations can all impact the career trajectories of the people they describe. This means that when you're giving any kind of recommendation, you should show complete confidence. No hedging ("she might be good"), faint praise ("she'll do okay"), or other phrases that undermine ("she needs only minimal guidance").

Wondering why I'm calling this out? Turns out that in a 2018 study of recommendations for academic positions, researchers found that letters about women included more doubt-raising phrases than those about men, and that even one such phrase can make a difference in a job search.[198] This means that a lukewarm recommendation may be more harmful than no recommendation at all.

After sharing this research on Twitter, I heard from Tom Hartley, who wrote:[199]

Tom Hartley @tom_hartley · Oct 8, 2018   ○○○
Reading some of my draft references, I sometimes think that even a solitary 'but' (connecting two otherwise unambiguously positive sentences) is enough to introduce doubt...

> **𝕽 Better Allies®** @betterallies · Oct 7, 2018
> When giving recommendations, I check myself for "doubt raisers" - phrases that unintentionally surface doubt. Like "She needs only minimal guidance" and "it's true that she doesn't have much experience."
>
> Study shows we give them to women more than men: hbr.org/2018/09/how-we...

♡ 1   ↻ 1   ♡ 3   ⬆

Tom Hartley @tom_hartley · Oct 8, 2018   ○○○
e.g., "X is an outstanding scientist but also a brilliant writer." Compare with "X is an outstanding scientist and brilliant writer".

♡   ↻   ♡ 6   ⬆

The next time you give someone a recommendation, make it a wholehearted one. Focus on the person's traits and accomplishments that are overwhelmingly positive and praise them to the skies. Otherwise, you risk shutting a door you intended to open.

Promoting on potential

Effective allies recognize and nurture raw talent in *all* of their employees. Research from both McKinsey and Lean In found that "men get promoted based on potential and women get promoted based on performance."[200] This means that women are stuck on a treadmill, constantly proving and reproving that they're worthy of responsibility and capable of leadership. In fact, when women did all the things they were told would help them get ahead — using the same tactics as men — they still advanced less than their male counterparts and had slower pay growth.[201]

This tendency illustrates what's known as "prove it again" bias. (You may remember from Chapter 10 that this bias also shows up in the hiring process.) Groups that have been stereotyped as less competent or hardworking often have to provide a larger, more compelling body of evidence in order to be judged as equally competent. Groups that have to "prove it again" include women, Black people, Latinx people, individuals with disabilities, and Asian Americans. While a white man may only need to show promise in order to secure a promotion, a Latina employee may need to make a long and convincing case for herself to even be considered for advancement. Members of "prove it again" groups are often labeled as "not ready" for promotion, which can be code for unconscious bias. When promoting managers find themselves describing certain candidates as "not ready," they should consider whether they're expecting those folks to provide more evidence of competence.[202]

More evidence that men are immune from "prove it again" bias: They're more likely to get what they want without even having to ask. According to the 2017 "Women in the Workplace" study:

Women of all races and ethnicities negotiate for raises and promotions at rates comparable to their male counterparts. However, men are more likely to say they have not asked for a raise because they are already well compensated or a promotion because they are already in the right role.[203]

While women are repeatedly asked to illustrate competence through performance, men get access to advancement opportunities without having to ask for them. While women must prove their worth, men are promoted simply for showing potential.

So how do allies recognize potential in their employees, regardless of gender, background, or identity? How can allies combat "prove it again" bias and learn to see promise in their colleagues and direct reports?

Psychologists Tomas Chamorro-Premuzic and Seymour Adler, along with leadership author Robert B. Kaiser, found that traits like enthusiasm and success-centric mindsets are considered desirable by corporate leaders, but don't actually indicate that an employee has high potential. Their study showed that the following three markers of high potential are the ones to look for:

- **Ability.** Is the candidate capable of doing the job in question? Is the candidate clearly able to learn and master the requisite knowledge and skills needed to perform this job?
- **Social skills.** Does the candidate excel at teamwork and collaboration? Can the candidate manage both themself and others?
- **Drive.** Is the candidate willing to work hard, achieve, and do whatever it takes to get the job done?[204]

Clearly, people of all genders and backgrounds can possess all three of these traits. "Ability" only becomes dicey if a promoting manager insists that a certain candidate prove again and again that they have what it takes. If you are an ally who is hoping to evaluate an employee from an underrepresented group for a promotion, consider these three criteria instead of relying entirely on your gut. (Guts can be biased!) And if you are in a position to sit on a calibration or promotions board, and you don't know all of the candidates, take the time to get to know them. Once you do, find ways to scope and recognize their potential instead of insisting they prove their worthiness through performance.

How a simple nudge can open a door

In *Work Rules!*, Laszlo Bock describes a problem Google was facing: Women employees were less likely to nominate themselves for promotions, despite a policy that allowed all employees to do so.[205] The company found that a small nudge made a huge difference. All it took was senior vice president Alan Eustace sending an email to employees citing research about classroom dynamics, where boys tend to raise their hand to answer any question, where girls tend to wait to be certain. With that nudge, not only did application rates from women soar, the volume of their promotions even surpassed those of their male counterparts.[206]

Allies don't need to be in a position to directly promote marginalized employees. Think about providing support from the sidelines. Just encouraging them, nudging them to push forward in their careers, can make a huge difference.

Layers of bias can form doorstops

In 2018, the Kapor Center ran a pilot study on the challenges facing women tech entrepreneurs, including the myriad biases women face when raising capital. The researchers also studied how race factors in, with women of color reporting substantially worse experiences than white women. One statistic caught my eye: "Women of color were more than 3 times as likely to report bullying than white women (75% versus 22%), and nearly 10 times as likely to report experiencing non-consensual touching (38% vs 4%)."[207] Let that sink in. It's a not-so-subtle reminder that intersectionality must be taken into account when we create promotion strategies and diversification efforts.

As you think about how to open career doors, realize that not all women face the same challenges, and that women of color may need different support and allyship because of the additional and compounded bias and harassment they confront.

One last thing

In 2017, Jill Wetzler, then a director of engineering at Lyft, gave an inspiring conference talk titled "The Inclusive Leader: Developing Diverse Teams."[208] One of the many excellent tips she gave was to encourage attendees to sponsor protégés who are not like them.

Think about who you sponsor. If they tend to be "like you" or remind you of your younger self, consider developing relationships with a more diverse group of coworkers — and start opening some doors for them. Speak their name when they aren't around. Endorse them publicly. Invite them to high-profile meetings. Share their career goals with decision makers. Recommend them for stretch assignments and speaking opportunities.

In other words, be their champion.

5 THINGS (ALLIES) CAN DO TO (SPONSOR) COWORKERS FROM (UNDERREPRESENTED) GROUPS

SPEAK THEIR NAME WHEN THEY AREN'T AROUND

ENDORSE THEM PUBLICLY

INVITE THEM TO HIGH-PROFILE MEETINGS

SHARE THEIR CAREER GOALS WITH DECISION-MAKERS

RECOMMEND THEM FOR STRETCH ASSIGNMENTS AND SPEAKING OPPORTUNITIES

@BETTERALLIES

BETTERALLIES.COM

Actions for Better Allies:
Don't Be a Gatekeeper, Be a Door Opener

Helping people from underrepresented groups achieve their goals and advance their careers is one of the most powerful things allies can do. Here's how:

- Ask the people you manage or mentor about their career goals and, with permission, share them with decision makers.
- Be equitable when handing out stretch assignments and other learning opportunities.
- Give wholehearted recommendations and referrals.
- Advocate effectively during performance calibration meetings and promotion discussions.
- Nudge colleagues from marginalized groups to pursue career growth opportunities.
- Create a culture where accomplishments are regularly recognized and celebrated.
- Sponsor people who are not like you. Speak their name when they aren't around. Endorse them publicly. Invite them to high-profile meetings. Recommend them for stretch assignments and speaking opportunities.

13

A CALL TO ACTION

In August 2017, we recorded another milestone on the unofficial "lousy workplace diversity timeline" — a timeline that is all too full of events about sexism, bias, misogyny, creepy behavior, and harassment. It's a timeline that shouldn't exist, but does.

That's when Google engineer James Damore wrote an internal memo criticizing his company's diversity and inclusion efforts. In the ten-page screed, he argued that differences in pay between men and women in the technology sector are not rooted in bias against women but instead are attributable to biological differences between the genders.[209] In doing so, he made plenty of people angry, but also validated the secretly held beliefs of others: that diversity efforts are pointless, that women simply aren't good scientists, and that the best will rise to the top naturally. And that the best are men — usually white men.

When the story of his memo broke over the weekend, social media channels lit up. Myriad posts. Twitter fistfights. Blogged responses. Attention from the press. I couldn't pull myself away.

That said, I also found it draining. And I started to realize the challenge that women across the tech industry would face as they returned to work on Monday morning. Wondering if any of their teammates agreed with that memo, in part or in full. Wondering if they would need to debate their right to their chosen profession.

Unfortunately, more milestones get added to this unofficial "lousy workplace diversity timeline" periodically. Not long after the Google manifesto, #MeToo became a full-fledged movement with repercussions in multiple fields. Despite the fact that women held a mere 18 percent of all physics doctoral degrees in 2017, physicist Alessandro Strumia of the University of Pisa delivered a presentation explaining how the field of physics discriminates against men.[210] In 2018, Black scientist Raven Baxter moved from the corporate world to academia, and on her first day of work, a colleague threatened to call the cops on her.[211] Also in 2018, Stuart Reges, a University of Washington computer science lecturer, argued that women would never make up more than 20 percent of tech employees, likely because boys are better at math and science, and girls are better at reading.[212] There was only one Black executive among the leadership teams at Microsoft, Facebook, Google, Apple, and Amazon in 2019. He was at Google, and he left in January 2020.[213]

The list goes on.

And, of course, biases against underrepresented groups remain prevalent in fields besides tech. Consider how Serena Williams was treated at the 2018 U.S. Open finals, where she was penalized for expressing her frustration on the court. Multiple male tennis players came forward to say they'd said and done much worse during their matches and never been criticized. Management scholar and author Adam Grant summed it up perfectly by saying, "When a man argues with an umpire, it's passion. When a woman does it, it's a meltdown. When a Black woman does it, it's a penalty."[214]

In fact, since the killings of Breonna Taylor and George Floyd in 2020, more allies are becoming aware of a timeline that their Black colleagues are being forced to follow: that of the pain and fear they face whenever there is another high-profile incident of police brutality. That pain and fear inevitably shows up in the workplace. While white allies may feel many emotions in response to these acts of violence, Black people report feeling constantly and relentlessly traumatized. DEI advocate Michelle Kim points out,

> If you are able to disengage and not think about these issues, recognize you have privilege. If you're able to write off these issues as 'political' rather than personal, recognize you have privilege. Many people who are directly or indirectly impacted do not have the option to "turn off" nor call it "too political" to be discussed or felt in the workplace.[215]

Corey Ponder, who we heard from back in Chapter 2, summarizes this fraught experience by saying:

> I am proud to be black. And also, being black is exhausting. Every time another black person dies at the hands of police officers, it is a reminder of the leash that comes with my blackness. ... It's like being reminded that there are things in this society that I don't have clearance for, and access to the little I have can be taken away at a moment's notice ... It's best to be stoic: to learn patience through pain and resilience through wrongs. Except, stoicism usually means that only I sit with and process the trauma; only I am doing the work of figuring out the next steps and what it looks like to move forward. Meanwhile, time marches on, and when righting an injustice, time always feels like it is on the side of the unjust. That stinging reminder is a perpetual cycle of fatigue and frustration that spirals down into hopelessness.[216]

The Black Lives Matter movement continues to mobilize protests and demand action. But the violence against Black people also continues, and it impacts the lives and well-being of Black workers everywhere.

Incidents of victim blaming and character assassination remain widespread as well. It seems that little has changed since 1991, when Anita Hill accused Clarence Thomas of harassment during his U.S. Supreme Court hearings. We saw history repeat itself with Dr. Christine Blasey Ford's brave testimony against Brett Kavanaugh in 2018. Setting aside political leanings, there's an underlying cautionary tale for better allies everywhere: to not blame colleagues or assassinate their character when they raise issues or file formal complaints.

Chances are, more examples have been added to this timeline since I published this book. Sometimes, the struggle for equity in the workplace can feel like taking two steps forward only to be forced three steps back. But there are things allies can and should do to surge ahead.

Speak up and speak out

With each incident of inequity, allies have an opportunity to support colleagues who are more impacted than themselves. Effective allies not only say that they believe in these colleagues, but they also demonstrate it and show them that they think differently than the author of a leaked memo, the administrator in charge of a harmful policy, or the biased thought leader.

Allies have a duty to speak up, speak out, and take action. Here are some ideas on how to do so:

- Tell coworkers that you believe in workplace diversity and you're glad to be working with or for them.

- Express gratitude to coworkers, calling out specific behaviors you appreciate. For example, "I like the way you describe architectural risk during code reviews."
- Talk about specific things you've learned from coworkers. For example, "What I learned from Jada about AI open source libraries is ..."
- Tell coworkers about the expertise you see in them and how awesome they are.
- Challenge biased behavior when you see it. Don't be a bystander, be an upstander. Take action.
- Advocate for systemic changes to address noninclusive behavior. Don't act only as a knight to "save" one marginalized person. Instead, drive change that will help all marginalized individuals and create a more inclusive culture.

Commit to sponsoring four people

Toward the end of 2017, author and management expert Tom Peters tweeted, "Bosses: Who are the four folks whose development path you will have dramatically affected by 12/31/18?"[217] Unable to resist such a perfect setup, I replied, "Plot twist: Who are the four women or underrepresented humans whose development path you will have dramatically affected by 12/31/18? #MaleAllies."

My challenge to allies is to identify four women or members of other underrepresented groups to sponsor in the current or coming year. And by sponsor, I mean do things like:

- Speak their name when they're not around.
- Share their career goals with influencers.
- Recommend them for stretch assignments.
- Talk about what you've learned from them.

- Invite them to high-profile meetings.
- Give them your speaking slot at an event.
- Endorse them publicly.

Even if mentoring feels like an overwhelming time commitment at this point, you can start by sponsoring or even micro-sponsoring. Being visible and vocal in your support of those with less privilege and access is leading by example.

Start a ripple effect

In the late 1980s, my manager, Norm Meyrowitz, came back from a visit to Microsoft with a memorable story. During a meeting around a large conference table, he was surprised to see that everyone leaned back in their chairs with their arms behind their heads. Afterward, he asked his host, "What's up with Microsoft employees? Why do they all sit this way?" His host laughed and replied, "Because that's the way Bill sits in meetings."

That story has stuck with me ever since. It's a simple example of a ripple effect. Of how people mimic behavior (good or bad) that they see in others whom they respect.

In fact, I shared it recently when I was on a video call with someone at Microsoft. We were talking about how acts of allyship can cause a ripple effect, encouraging others to act in similar ways. The Bill Gates story was just too good not to bring up. As I relayed it, I noticed the other person was smiling. She went on to tell me that in her first one-on-one meeting at Microsoft, about seven years ago, her boss also "sat like Bill." He leaned back in his chair, arms behind his head, and he even put his feet up on his desk.

Now get this … Gates left his day-to-day operations role in 2008. That means his ripple effect was still having an impact five years later when this person joined the company. (I'm sure he's had a lasting impact on the culture beyond just the way people sit, but that's beyond the scope of this book.)

As David Smith and Brad Johnson wrote in *Good Guys,*

> Remember all those junior men around you. They're always watching. When a male ally speaks up, he's not only effecting change in the room at that moment, he's inviting and empowering the next generation of men ... And that is how we change a culture.[218]

Being an ally is a journey, and you don't have to do it all at once. Start with a single act. While it may seem small, you'll make a difference. You may even start a ripple effect.

Own and apologize for your mistakes

If you make a mistake, apologize, learn, and take action. Like all humans, you're imperfect and bound to mess up once in a while. When you make a mistake, don't double down on your stance. Instead, share a heartfelt apology and discuss how you can do better.

Here's an example of a mistake I made that I want to share with you. During Black History Month, I tweeted:[219]

Better Allies® @betterallies · Feb 6, 2019   ○○○

During #BlackHistoryMonth ✊🏿, my goal as a white person is to take actions that will last year-round:
☞ Select books by POC authors to read during 2019
☞ Offer to be a mentor to folks in our POC employee group
☞ Identify events for POC to attend this year (where I'll be welcome)

♡ 1   ⟲   ♡ 10   ⬆

You'll notice that I wrote "POC" (for Person of Color) instead of "Black." Katrina Jones, Head of Diversity and Inclusion at Twitch, immediately replied:[220]

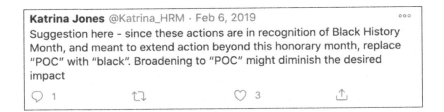

I'm grateful to Jones for pointing this out. I learned from her, thanked her, and took action by tweeting an improved version.

Define or refresh your values

Although I want this book to focus on actions that stretch allies beyond thinking, there is definitely a place in this call-to-action chapter for self-reflection. Change starts with each of us as individuals. So, we should ask ourselves: How do we want to operate? How should we treat people? Would we turn down business or investments because of creepy behavior? Would we dismiss our top sales executive after disciplining him for harassment? What are the deals we won't do because they conflict with our values? When will we walk away from cash?

How allies treat colleagues from marginalized groups in the workplace must stretch beyond meeting protocols and everyday language, and toward activities that impact the bottom line. Allyship becomes meaningless if it's abandoned in the face of lucrative business deals or strategic partnerships. Committed allies remember their values and live them out.

Continue the journey

I firmly believe that you don't have to be a manager or have the words "Diversity," "Inclusion," or "Belonging" on your business card to make a difference. There are everyday actions we all can take to create more inclusive workplaces. There are myriad ways we can be allies.

This book is just one resource, and I hope you've found it helpful. I also have a weekly newsletter, "5 Ally Actions," where I share ideas curated from the week's news and my interactions with clients, audience members, and Twitter users from around the world. I'm on a mission myself to be a better ally, and I learn new approaches all the time. My goal is to share my learnings and to bring others along with me through this newsletter. You can subscribe at *www.betterallies.com*.

If you prefer social media, I'd love to have you follow @betterallies on Twitter, Instagram, Medium, or Pinterest.

Being an ally is a journey, and I'm thrilled that you're joining me. Together, we can — and will — make a difference.

BONUS CHAPTER

INTERVIEWING WHILE WHITE AND MALE

Steve Tannock, a technology architect, asked me this question: "Perfectly selfishly: I'm a middle-aged white guy who generally only wants to work with/for orgs doing good diversity work. But hiring me is almost the opposite of that. Suggestions for reconciling/approaching this?"

Many people with privilege feel the same way as Tannock. If this is you, here are five suggestions, not only to help you land that next job but *also* to further diversity, equity, and inclusion along the way.

Emphasize what you've done to build and support diverse teams

Kristen Pressner, a global HR executive who speaks about the power of #FlipItToTestIt, had this advice for Tannock and others in positions of privilege because of their race, gender, or other factors: "Flip it from assuming that you don't have a 'diversity value' to what value you can add. Emphasize what you've done in the past to build diverse teams and how you've supported them to be successful."[221]

I love this suggestion. Not only does it allow a candidate to shine a positive light on their past experience, it could also give the interviewers an idea or two about how *they* could become better allies. Win-win!

Talk about your dedication to mentoring colleagues from underrepresented groups

David Smith, coauthor of *Athena Rising* and *Good Guys*, provided this advice for Tannock: "Gender inclusion is not a women's issue to solve — it is the organization's issue. Share how you've mentored and sponsored women and how you'll continue to do so in your next role."[222]

This is especially important in the context and aftermath of the #MeToo movement. Men shouldn't retreat from mentoring women. Ditto for mentoring members of other under-represented groups. We need everyone working in support of diversity and inclusion.

Know your diversity adversity story

Even if you check lots of privilege checkboxes, you've probably faced some adversity. Jennifer Brown, author of *Inclusion* and *How to Be an Inclusive Leader*, recommends: "Identify your diversity story — about a time you faced the sting of exclusion. Be vulnerable. Share it to model the value you place on inclusive workplace practices."[223]

One example of this is a senior leader who had been covering up the fact that he didn't hold a college degree. Once he started sharing this story, he became more approachable and eventually served as a role model for alternative education paths for his employees.

Now for a note of caution. Don't use your diversity adversity story as a "get out of jail free pass." Realize that your privilege as a white man has allowed you to navigate your career in a way that is far different than those from underrepresented demographics. Acknowledge that you have it easy by comparison and that you feel a responsibility to drive change.

Ask what the company is doing to create an inclusive workplace

Interviewing is a two-way street. Be sure to ask the interview team about why diversity and inclusion are important to them, and what the company is doing in this area. Cath Jones, a people operations professional, shared this advice for Tannock:

> I always find it valuable to ask what policies and processes they have in place. If they are heading down the right track they will be thinking about things like inclusion, the gender pay gap, physical accessibility of the office, etc. If not, you can normally gauge by [their] response how open they are to improvement. We need people at the top to guide the way and advocate for others. A good organisation won't have an issue that you aren't a minority but they will want to know that you share their values.[224]

If you join that company, you'll be in a position to check that it's actually living its values — that it's committed to offering an inclusive workplace. And you can hold leaders accountable if they're straying from that goal.

Be vulnerable and share a mistake you made on your journey to be a better ally (and what you learned from it)

We've all been there. Wanting to show our support for diversity, but saying the wrong thing. Or writing a quick message and using gendered language by mistake. Or laughing at an off-color joke. You know what I'm talking about. Perhaps you've been a bystander who ignored some racist, sexist or otherwise offensive behavior, and in hindsight, you know you should have called it out.

Turns out there's a growing number of veterans using #IWasWrong to share how they were complicit in the culture of misogyny in the U.S. Armed Forces.

As you prep for your next interview, think about your #IWasWrong story. A time when you were complicit, when you didn't take action to support someone from a marginalized group, when you didn't push back against noninclusive behaviors. Think about what you learned from that experience about how to be a better ally. It's a great way to answer the classic interview question, "Tell me about a time you made a mistake, and how you handled it."

One last thing

For those of you on the other side of the interview table, be sure to ask candidates about how they've contributed to creating a more inclusive workplace. And if you're interviewing them for a management role, ask about prior experience building and leading diverse teams, as discussed in Chapter 6.

EPILOGUE

THE BINGO CARD THAT STARTED IT ALL

I did not attend the Grace Hopper Celebration in 2014. Instead, I watched the keynotes that were streamed online, and I followed along on social media.

In the days leading up to the event, a buzz started building on Twitter about the male allies panel that was a scheduled feature of the conference. Complaints were surfacing about men taking the stage away from women at a women's conference, and questions were raised. If these panelists were such great allies for women, why didn't their companies have better diversity?

And then I saw a tweet that caught my eye.

A group calling themselves "The Union of Concerned Feminists" created a bingo card with phrases they expected to hear from the panelists, phrases that would show that these men still had a long journey ahead of them before they became true male allies.[225] They handed out the bingo card to the audience. And about halfway through the panel, a young woman shouted out, "Bingo."

A L L Y   B I N G O

We are glad that men are talking about supporting women in tech. But GHC is already full of women! Being an ally means confronting oppressive behavior *when you're around people in the majority group*, not explaining to a bunch of women how *totally* not sexist you are, and how your company has changed (we're looking at you, GoDaddy, and your multi-billion-dollar IPO aspirations). With that, we present to you many of the things you are about to hear in this panel, because we've heard it all before. BINGO TIME!

Name drops Sheryl Sandberg	"That would never happen in my company"	Calls a woman articulate	Refers to a feminist as aggressive / angry / offputting	Blames "awkward geeks" for abusive behavior in tech
Wearables. Women like wearing things, right?	"Ask any woman I know, she'll tell you I'm a feminist"	Teaches girls to code but won't mentor women	Quotes woman he has power over in the workplace	Ignorant of employment equity legislation
Corporate redemption narrative	Wants a cookie for basic decency	~~PIPELINE~~	"I asked a woman and she agreed with me"	Asserts other man's heart is in the right place
"I am related to a woman" / Saw the light after birth of daughter	"If GoDaddy can change, anyone can"	Says feminist activism scares women away from tech	My mother taught me to respect women	"I've believed in women's rights my whole life"
"We're all in this together"	"Men's voices need to be heard too"	Quotes MLK, gets meaning reversed	"I consider myself an equalist / humanist"	Lean In

During the Q&A session, here are some suggestions for questions to ask of these dudes:

- Have you conducted a pay equity audit, and if so, what were the results?
- How do your rates of promotion compare between women and men?
- Which efforts to reduce sexism at your company target men's behavior?
- What programs specific to retaining women do you have in place at your company?

This intervention brought to you by the **Union of Concerned Feminists**. Find us on Twitter at **@ConcernedFems**. Read more about actual feminism in technology, not the milquetoast corporate "feminism" you saw today, from some of our friends:

modelviewculture.com   geekfeminism.org   geekfeminism.wikia.com   adainitiative.org

Reprinted with permission of Leigh Honeywell

The bingo card was a hit. Perhaps because it highlighted that diversity initiatives are so often trite sound bites backed by minimal action. After all, three of the four companies represented on the panel had an employee pool in which fewer than twenty percent of the technical staff were women, so clearly they had a long way to go.

That said, I wondered if these men (and other men working across tech) would ever figure out how to be better allies.

I decided to make an aspirational version. A bingo card with phrases I *wanted* to hear from men. Phrases that show they are taking a stand to improve diversity and not just paying lip service to it. Phrases that represented actions they could take to make a difference.

To make the bingo card, I partnered with another technologist, Cate Huston, who was at the panel and became heavily involved in pushing back against it, which led to a well-received "reverse panel" the next day for the men to listen to women's concerns. Together, Cate and I wrote and rewrote a series of aspirational phrases, editing and culling our list, and used an online bingo card generator to create the card.

I speak at conferences only if they have a code of conduct.	We did a salary review by gender and corrected inequities.	We track retention numbers of women in our engineering roles.	I publically recognize & reward women who are involved with helping other women.	We have published goals for improving our diversity numbers.
Our job descriptions include "experience working on a diverse team, with a diverse range of people."	I proactively work to amplify more women's voices.	I have a zero-tolerance policy of derogatory language in design documents and in code.	I refuse invitations to all-male panels.	Gender diversity is more than a just pipeline problem.
I have spoken up when women are discriminated against or excluded from activities.	I have banned the phrase "Hiring Bar."	I am a feminist	Our job descriptions list only required skills, not nice-to-haves.	We proactively address biased feedback in interviews and promotion cycles.
Our job descriptions list open source experience only when it is a true requirement.	We track time in role and promotion rates for underrepresented minorities.	I meet with women who file HR complaints so that I can understand the issues and support them.	I have encouraged other men to speak up when minorities are discriminated against or belittled in front of them.	I have been a sponsor to a woman.
I have been a peer mentor to a woman.	I have recommended a qualified women for opportunities I could not pursue myself.	I have invested in a female founder.	I have fired a person with privilege or power for being sexist.	I have read extensively including peer reviewed literature on unconscious bias.

Once it was done, we wanted to share it with the world. Cate secured a web domain to host it, and I started tweeting the phrases from a new Twitter account, @betterallies. Then we wrote about it for the *Daily Beast* in an article titled "Tech's Male 'Feminists' Aren't Helping."[226]

Soon after we published that article, Kathryn Rotondo reached out, offering to edit and redesign the bingo card. I'm forever grateful for the work she did to turn our ugly duckling into this stunning design:

This project was my catalyst, the starting point on my journey for both editions of this book. And I'm deeply grateful to Cate Huston for partnering with me to create the bingo card, Kathryn Rotondo for her design and editing work, and Leigh Honeywell, the person behind the original bingo card at the 2014 Grace Hopper Celebration, for instigating it all.[227]

You can download the bingo card from *www.betterallies.com*. Consider printing it and posting it in a visible area of your workplace to generate awareness. Or hand it out at an event, like Suzanne Axtell frequently did when she was working at O'Reilly Media's technical conferences.

Interested in creating a bingo card for allies in your industry? Our design is offered under the Creative Commons Attribution 4.0 International license, which means you can distribute, remix, tweak, and build upon it as long as you credit us for the original creation, like The 3% Movement did in creating a "Manbassador Bingo Card" for the 2015 3% Conference in London.[228] Be sure to tell me if you make one by sending an email to info@betterallies.com or tagging @betterallies on Twitter. I'd love to see your creation.

Our journey continues.

RECAP: ACTIONS FOR BETTER ALLIES

Here's a compilation of the actions included at the end of each chapter.

Understand Your Privilege and Use It for Good

An important part of allyship is being open to learning, improving, and taking action.

- Review the list of fifty potential privileges in the workplace that was included in this chapter. How many apply to you?
- Identify at least one way you can be a better ally, using the archetypes in this chapter.
- Understand that being an ally is a journey. We all make mistakes. Don't let that hold you back from taking action. Don't opt out.

Be an Ambassador for Change

Helping individuals is laudable, but the responsibility of allies is to take actions that will have lasting, beneficial effects on systems (as often as possible).

- When lending a hand to a single person, step back to look for systemic changes that will benefit many employees.
- Suggest new processes that will change ingrained behaviors and create a more inclusive culture.
- Pay attention to your motivations: Focus on what will authentically support marginalized people over the long-term, rather than what will make you feel or look good.

Listen, Believe, Learn

Being an effective ally includes the less forceful but equally important activities of listening to alternate perspectives, accepting the information that people from underrepresented groups share, and learning from their stories and one's own mistakes.

- Be vulnerable and honest when you open discussions with colleagues who have less power and privilege than you.
- Resist the urge to get defensive.
- Review the list of red-flag phrases that was included in Chapter 3, and speak out when you hear them.
- Take action when you see or hear about bigotry, harassment, or discrimination. Be an upstander, not a bystander.
- Accept that yes, prejudice does exist in your own workplace.

Diversify Your Network

Most of us have largely homogeneous networks. Here are some tips for ensuring that your network is diverse and more effective:

- Do a network inventory. List out the people you feel to be your top ten contacts. Are any of them marginalized in ways that you are not? If not, start in your own backyard: Who within your own organization could be a great addition to your current network?
- Attend an event where diversity will be the topic of discussion. Listen and learn.

- The next time you attend an event of *any* kind, introduce yourself to someone who doesn't look like you.
- If you are interested in attending an event that caters specifically to a group of which you are not a member, ask the organizers before showing up.
- Seek out media, including podcasts and blogs, by people who are different from you.

Make Events Welcoming

Too many professional events can be inhospitable for members of underrepresented groups. Here are some ways to help turn the tide:

- Make events inclusive. Feature diverse voices, offer interesting nonalcoholic drinks, create and enforce a code of conduct, practice full accessibility, provide financial assistance, and push back on risqué images and offensive swag.
- Before attending or agreeing to speak at an event, make sure there will be a code of conduct as well as other support for attendees from underrepresented groups.
- If you see a lineup of speakers that's homogeneous, contact the organizers and demand better.
- Look out for microaggressions (or worse) during an event, and take action when you spot them.

Amplify and Advocate in Meetings

In many organizations, much of the workday is spent in meetings. This means that ensuring the voices of members of underrepresented groups are heard and valued is essential to creating an inclusive work culture.

- Challenge yourself to notice and take action when interruptions happen in meetings.
- Cultivate a culture of credit: Encourage everyone around you to acknowledge the originator of ideas as often as possible.
- Be vigilant and push back on off-topic questions and showboating.
- Take note of how attendees arrange themselves in meeting rooms. Do what you can to mix up seating arrangements so your marginalized coworkers are in power positions.
- Ask a back-channel buddy to keep you accountable.
- Don't insist that people turn on their video cameras for virtual meetings.

Share the Load

Office housework isn't just aggravating. Calling exclusively on women, BIPOC, and members of other marginalized groups to perform it means preventing them from tackling more meaningful work. With that in mind:

- Share the work among the team. For example, if you notice one person is always tasked with mentoring the summer interns, say something like, "Ann's great at mentoring. But it's the perfect stretch assignment for Jacob, who has never done it before."

- Set up a rotation for tasks like taking minutes or scheduling the next meeting.
- If you're in a position of privilege or authority, model better behavior yourself by clearing the lunch leftovers or used coffee mugs, rather than assuming someone else will take care of it.
- Never assume that certain coworkers are shouldering office housework because they "enjoy" it or find it "rewarding."

Watch Your Words

As Security Nerdette pointed out in her Twitter thread, "How we spend our day is how we spend our life." It may seem like word choice is a minor issue, but it's one that accumulates over time.

- Be aware and respectful of pronouns, gendered language, and phrases that are demeaning or offensive. Lead by example in how you use (or don't use) both.
- Take time to learn people's names and how to pronounce them.
- Create a safe space for people in your workplace or industry to ask questions and discuss problematic language.
- Be aware that some terms you think are innocuous may be harmful to others. If you mess up, apologize.

Share Speaking Opportunities

Allies who are truly dedicated to amplifying marginalized voices must be willing to give up a few choice speaking gigs so others may share their knowledge.

- If you're a man and are asked to speak as part of an all-male lineup, push back and/or decline.
- If you're white, say no to all-white panels.
- When you do present, ensure that your slide images show people from a variety of backgrounds, gender identities, body types, and abilities.
- If you're offered a speaking engagement but know someone from an underrepresented group who could knock it out of the park, connect them to the event organizer and pass on the spot yourself.

Strive to Hire Equitably

Allies can band together to banish the "leaky pipeline" excuses and focus on employing strategies that are proven to attract and hire applicants from underrepresented groups. Here are some ways you can make this possible in your organization:

- Ensure that your company's careers web page uses language and images to convey that people from marginalized groups are welcome and belong in your workplace.
- Create interview processes and teams that will set up candidates for success, and prep interviewers to be aware of hidden biases.
- Implement structured interviews for open positions.
- Evaluate candidates on their inclusion experience, using the suggested questions in this chapter.

- Emphasize that employees were hired because they were highly qualified, to combat any concern that they're just a "diversity hire."

Give Effective and Equitable Feedback

Feedback can be tricky to give, but it truly is a gift to receive. Without clear feedback, members of marginalized groups will have a much harder time succeeding and advancing. So, as an ally, remember:

- When giving feedback, focus on the business impact of an employee's work. What should they keep doing because it's moving the business forward? How should they improve in order to have an even bigger impact?
- Don't ease up just to avoid hurt feelings. Remember, vague feedback holds people back from growing in their careers.
- Tell them about the expertise you see in them and how to develop more job-related skills.
- Use objective criteria to evaluate employees in similar roles.
- Write reviews of roughly the same length for everyone on your staff.
- Ask for feedback on how you can be a better ally.

Don't Be a Gatekeeper, Be a Door Opener

Helping people from underrepresented groups achieve their goals and advance their careers is one of the most powerful things allies can do. Here's how:

- Ask the people you manage or mentor about their career goals and, with permission, share them with decision makers.
- Be equitable when handing out stretch assignments and other learning opportunities.
- Give wholehearted recommendations and referrals.
- Advocate effectively during performance calibration meetings and promotion discussions.
- Nudge colleagues from marginalized groups to pursue career growth opportunities.
- Create a culture where accomplishments are regularly recognized and celebrated.
- Sponsor people who are not like you. Speak their name when they aren't around. Endorse them publicly. Invite them to high-profile meetings. Recommend them for stretch assignments and speaking opportunities.

DISCUSSION GUIDE

Allyship is considerably more daunting when attempted alone. If you're looking for a next-step activity that can connect you to other like-minded colleagues, coworkers, and friends, consider forming a discussion group on this book.

Here are questions to consider. Some require pre-work, so send them to participants ahead of time. You can download a PDF of this discussion guide at *www.betterallies.com*.

Icebreaker: How would you complete this sentence? "I want a more diverse and inclusive workplace because _____ ."

Question 1: How well do you know your own privilege? Using the list in Chapter 1, examine your privilege. As you review this list, keep a tally. Note any items that surprise you and make you wonder, "Does anyone actually face this challenge?" Discuss these items with the group.

Question 2: Discuss a recent experience in which you saw discriminatory or inappropriate behavior and didn't step in or speak up. What held you back? Do you feel more equipped to intervene now?

Question 3: In Chapter 1, you'll find descriptions of roles that allies can play. Which one sounds most like you? Which one do you admire most? If you were to push yourself to take on another ally role in addition to the one you play naturally, what would it be?

Question 4: Chapter 3 offers some advice for approaching challenging discussions around privilege, bias, and discrimination. Do you wish you could have one of these discussions with your supervisor, colleagues, or direct reports? What's the heart of the issue? How can you apply the guidelines offered in this chapter? Be honest, and ask for help and input from your fellow book club members.

Question 5: Think about your professional and personal networks. Are they "just like" you? Think about gaps and how a more diverse network could have a positive impact on your professional goals.

Question 6: Which microaggressions do you witness or experience on a regular basis? (See Chapter 5 for examples.)

Question 7: Think about your meeting culture. Do you regularly experience or witness idea hijacking, "manterruptions," showboating, or assignment of housework to women or other colleagues from underrepresented groups? What's one thing you can do in the coming week to shift the culture in a more inclusive direction?

Question 8: Chapter 8 is all about how seemingly harmless phrases and words can actually be insulting, discriminatory, and hurtful. Do any of the terms discussed in this chapter pop up at your own workplace? Do you feel comfortable stepping up and asking that they be eliminated or replaced?

Question 9: Of the industry events you've attended, which ones have showcased speakers and panels that felt inclusive and representative? Which ones disappointed you? When you consider attending a conference, do you screen the speakers ahead of time?

Question 10: Before the club meets, review the careers page on your company's website and a recent job description. Using the best practices in Chapter 10, identify ways you are set up to attract diverse candidates, and brainstorm ideas for improvement. If possible, bring them up on a laptop and discuss as a group.

Question 11: Are you now (or have you been) a mentor to someone with less experience? How about someone with less experience and a very different background, lifestyle, or identity than you?

Final Lightning Round: What action will you take going forward to create a more inclusive workplace? (Consider asking someone to be your "accountability buddy" to check in and help ensure that you make progress.)

ACKNOWLEDGMENTS

Even for an introvert like me, the process of writing a book is a lonely one. It involves many solo hours working on the outline, repurposing blog posts, drafting new chapters, researching, and editing — all of which are engrossing and enriching activities but tough to do in total isolation. In fact, after a while I found myself battling with a serious case of impostor syndrome. The critic inside my head questioned if the book I was writing would be helpful to anyone, and fretted over relevant research or points of view I was forgetting to include.

So, like most authors, I sought out support and input, and received a boatload of insight and reassurance. While what I've written is far from comprehensive, I do hope *Better Allies* is helpful to all who read it. And I want to thank all those who helped me make it happen.

First of all, a huge thank you to Tim and our children Emma and Ted. Not only did you cheer me on every step of the way, you also helped me brainstorm ideas, reviewed drafts, and proofread every word. This book was definitely a family effort!

I also want to thank Cate Huston, my collaborator on the bingo card that started it all. Would this book have come about if we hadn't first created that card and its diversity-driven affirmations for allies? I don't think so.

To my many supporters on social media, I'm forever grateful. Through your engagement with my handle @betterallies, I discovered which points resonated and I refined how I wanted to talk about allyship. With your positive reinforcement and invaluable insights, I developed my voice and found the courage to write this book.

I'm also grateful to every single person who shared a story with me. I wanted this book to include a multitude of perspectives and voices, and it is so much better as a result of your contributions.

To the reviewers who provided me with invaluable feedback on my manuscript (especially Norm and Joe) and those who wrote testimonials to help me spread the word about my book, many thanks!

And to Susan Fowler, whose blog post in February 2017 catalyzed conversations about the lack of inclusive cultures across tech, a heartfelt thank-you. You paved the way for authors like me.

Last but not least, to my writing partner, Sally McGraw: I couldn't have done it without you. Thank you so very much.

ADDITIONAL RESOURCES

Below are resources I've curated to help you be a better ally. Clickable versions of these resources are available online at *www.betterallies.com/resources*.

Stock Photography and Illustrations Featuring People From Underrepresented Groups

Black.illustrations

Illustrations of Black people for your next digital project. Many packs are free, some packs come with a small fee.
www.blackillustrations.com

Canva Natural Woman Collection

Images featuring everyday women who are as diverse as they are beautiful. While most are available for a fee, some are free.
www.canva.com/photos/natural-women

CreateHER Stock

Authentic stock images featuring melanated women. Some are freebies, others are available with a monthly subscription fee.
www.createherstock.com

The Disability Collection

Images that break stereotypes and authentically portray people with disabilities in everyday life. Available for a fee.
www.verizonmedia.com/accessibility/disability-collection

Gender Spectrum Collection

Free images of trans and nonbinary models that go beyond the clichés.
broadlygenderphotos.vice.com

Jopwell Collection

Free stock photos featuring Black, Latinx, and Native American students and professionals.

jopwellcollection.jopwell.com

Lean In Collection at Getty Images

Images devoted to the powerful depiction of women, girls and the people who support them. Available for a fee.

www.gettyimages.com/collections/leanin

Nappy

Beautiful, high-res photos of Black and Brown people. For free.

www.nappy.co

PhotoAbility

Images of people with differing abilities, available for a fee.

www.photoability.net

Queer in Tech

Free stock photos to promote the visibility of queer and gender-nonconforming people in technology.

www.flickr.com/photos/mapbox/albums/72157713100349311

TONL

Culturally diverse stock photos, available for a fee.

www.tonl.co

UKBlackTech

Free stock photos of Black people using technology.

www.ukblacktech.com/stockphotos

WOCintechchat

Free stock photos of women of color working in tech settings.

www.flickr.com/photos/wocintechchat

Articles on Using More Inclusive Language

"11 Common English Words And Phrases With Racist Origins" by Dylan Lyons.
www.babbel.com/en/magazine/common-racist-words-phrases

"70 Inclusive Language Principles That Will Make You A More Successful Recruiter" by Nehemiah Green.
www.medium.com/diversity-together/70-inclusive-language-principles-that-will-make-you-a-more-successful-recruiter-part-1-79b7342a0923

"100 Ways to Make the World Better for Non-binary People" by AC Dumlao.
broadly.vice.com/en_us/article/evkwm4/how-to-be-an-ally-to-non-binary-gender-non-conforming-people-support

"An Incomplete Guide to Inclusive Language for Startups and Tech" by Courtney Seiter.
www.buffer.com/resources/inclusive-language-tech/

"The Radical Copyeditor's Style Guide for Writing About Transgender People" by Alex Kapitan.
www.radicalcopyeditor.com/2017/08/31/transgender-style-guide/

"Use These Culturally Offensive Phrases, Questions at Your Own Risk" by Indigenous Corporate Training Inc.
www.ictinc.ca/blog/culturally-offensive-phrases-you-should-use-at

Source for an Inclusive Language Slackbot

www.betterallies.com/language/

ABOUT THE AUTHOR

Karen Catlin is a leadership coach and an acclaimed author and speaker on inclusive workplaces. After spending 25 years building software products and serving as a vice president of engineering at Macromedia and Adobe, she witnessed a sharp decline in the number of women working in tech. Frustrated but galvanized, she knew it was time to switch gears.

Today, Karen coaches women to be stronger leaders and men to be better allies. Her client roster includes Airbnb, DoorDash, eBay, Intel, and Intuit, as well as motivated entrepreneurs and individuals. Karen's coaching offerings include tactics for increasing visibility, being more strategic, managing stakeholders, negotiation, and cultivating ally skills. Her writing on these and related topics has appeared in *Inc.*, the *Daily Beast*, *Fast Company*, and *The Muse,* and she's consulted on articles for the *Wall Street Journal*, *Forbes*, and the *New York Times*. In late 2014, Karen started the Twitter handle @betterallies to share simple, actionable steps that anyone could take to make their workplaces more inclusive. She continues to tweet and blog for Better Allies, and she also emails a roundup of "5 Ally Actions" to her subscribers every week.

A self-professed public speaking geek, Karen is a highly sought-after and engaging presenter who has delivered talks at hundreds of conferences and corporate events. She speaks on a variety of topics, including inclusive workplaces and women in leadership. Her TEDx talk, "Women in Tech: The Missing Force," explores the decline in gender diversity in tech, why it's a problem, and what can be done about it. In addition to speaking herself, Karen is determined to change the ratio for who is on stage giving keynotes and other presentations. To support her goal of bringing more diversity to speaker lineups at tech industry events, she coauthored the book *Present! A Techie's Guide to Public Speaking* with Poornima Vijayashanker.

Karen is a graduate and active alum of Brown University, serving as an advisor to the university's Computer Science Diversity Initiative and mentoring students on how to launch their careers. She's also a member of the board of directors of DigitalNEST and on the advisory boards for the Women's CLUB of Silicon Valley and WEST (Women Entering & Staying in Technology). In 2015, the California State Assembly honored Karen with the Wonder Women Tech Innovator Award for outstanding achievements in business and technology and for being a role model for women.

Karen and her partner Tim live in San Mateo, California. They're the proud parents of Emma and Ted.

To find out what Karen's up to next, visit her website at *www.karencatlin.com.*

NOTES

Author's Note

1. John Daniszewski, "Why we will lowercase white," *AP*, July 20, 2020, https://blog.ap.org/announcements/why-we-will-lowercase-white.

2. Shereen Marisol Meraji and Natalie Escobar, "Is It Time To Say R.I.P. to 'POC'?," *NPR*, September 30, 2020, https://www.npr.org/2020/09/29/918418825/is-it-time-to-say-r-i-p-to-p-o-c.

Inroduction

3. Selena Larson, "Microsoft CEO Satya Nadella to Women: Don't Ask for a Raise, Trust Karma," *ReadWrite*, October 9, 2014, https://readwrite.com/2014/10/09/nadella-women-dont-ask-for-raise/.

4. Tanya Tarr, "By the Numbers: What Pay Inequality Looks Like for Women in Tech," *Forbes*, April 4, 2018, https://www.forbes.com/sites/tanyatarr/2018/04/04/by-the-numbers-what-pay-inequality-looks-like-for-women-in-tech/#2a7fbab860b1.

5. Selena Larson, "White Male 'Allies' Have Surprisingly Little to Say about Fixing Sexist Tech Culture," *ReadWrite*, October 9, 2014, https://readwrite.com/2014/10/09/technology-sexism-male-allies-grace-hopper-celebration/.

6. Buck Gee and Denise Peck, *The Illusion of Asian Success: Scant Progress for Minorities in Cracking the Glass Ceiling from 2007–2015* (New York: Ascend, 2017), https://c.ymcdn.com/sites/www.ascendleadership.org/resource/resmgr/research/TheIllusionofAsianSuccess.pdf.

7. Rani Molla, "It's Not Just Google—Many Major Tech Companies Are Struggling with Diversity," *Recode*, August 7, 2017, https://www.recode.net/2017/8/7/16108122/major-tech-companies-silicon-valley-diversity-women-tech-engineer.

8. Sam Levin, "What Happens When Tech Firms End Up at the Center of Racism Scandals?," *The Guardian*, August 30, 2016, https://www.theguardian.com/technology/2016/aug/30/tech-companies-racial-discrimination-nextdoor-airbnb.

9. "What Is Intersectionality?," Grinnell College, accessed October 1, 2018, http://haenfler.sites.grinnell.edu/subcultural-theory-and-theorists/intersectionality/.

Chapter 1: The Ally Journey

10. Kittu Pannu, "Privilege, Power, and Pride: Intersectionality Within the LGBT Community," *Impakter*, August 14, 2017, https://impakter.com/privilege-power-and-pride-intersectionality-within-the-lgbt-community/.

11. Kimberlé Crenshaw, "The Urgency of Intersectionality," filmed October 2016, TED video, 18:50, https://www.ted.com/talks/kimberle_crenshaw_the_urgency_of_intersectionality.

12. Sian Ferguson, "Privilege 101: A Quick and Dirty Guide," *Everyday Feminism*, September 29, 2014, https://everydayfeminism.com/2014/09/what-is-privilege/.

13. Andrew Grill, "I Gave Up My Seat at an All-Male Panel to a Woman—And More Men Should Do the Same," *Huffington Post*, May 27, 2015, https://www.huffingtonpost.com/andrew-grill/i-gave-up-my-seat-at-an-all-male-panel-to-a-woman_b_7451512.html.

14. Dorothy Pomerantz, "Driving Opportunity: GE's African American Forum Helps Its Members Rise — And Give Back," *GE*, Jan 17, 2020, https://www.ge.com/news/reports/driving-opportunity-ges-african-american-forum-helps-its-members-rise-and-give-back.

15. Susan Wojcicki, "Exclusive: How to Break Up the Silcon Valley Boys' Club," *Vanity Fair*, March 16, 2017, https://www.vanityfair.com/news/2017/03/how-to-break-up-the-silicon-valley-boys-club-susan-wojcicki.

16. Megan Carpenter, "Get it wrong for me: What I need from allies," *LinkedIn,* May 28, 2020, https://www.linkedin.com/pulse/get-wrong-me-what-i-need-from-allies-megan-carpenter/.

17. Brené Brown, *Dare to Lead* (New York: Random House, 2018).

Chapter 2: Knights versus Allies

18. Better Male Allies, "Male Allies: The Tech Industry Needs You," Opensource.com, June 13, 2017, https://opensource.com/article/17/6/male-allies-tech-industry-needs-you.

19. Jason van Gumster, "Haters Gonna Hate: 7 Ways to Deal with Criticism," Opensource.com, April 27, 2017, https://opensource.com/article/17/4/haters-gonna-hate.

20. Corey Ponder, "Allyship is Not the Hero's Journey," July 15, 2019, https://www.coreyponder.com/post/allyship-is-not-the-hero-s-journey.

21. Paul Kuttner, "The problem with that equity vs. equality graphic you're using," *Cultural Organizing blog*, November 1, 2016, https://culturalorganizing.org/the-problem-with-that-equity-vs-equality-graphic/.

Chapter 3: Listening and Learning

22. "Discussing Discrimination," American Psychological Association, accessed October 1, 2018, http://www.apa.org/helpcenter/keita-qa.aspx.

23. Dwight Smith, "The 8 R's of Talking about Race: How to Have Meaningful Conversations," *Net Impact*, June 18, 2015, https://www.netimpact.org/blog/the-8-r%E2%80%99s-of-talking-about-race-how-to-have-meaningful-conversations.

24. "Discussing Discrimination," American Psychological Association.

25. Dibs Baer, "11 Simple Ways You (Yes, You!) Can Make Your Workplace More LGBTQ Inclusive," *The Muse,* https://www.themuse.com/advice/simple-ways-make-workplace-more-lgbtq-inclusive.

26. "Ten Lessons for Talking about Race, Racism and Racial Justice," The Opportunity Agenda, February 23, 2017, https://opportunityagenda.org/explore/resources-publications/ten-lessons-talking-about-race-racism-and-racial-justice.

27. Robin DiAngelo, "How White People Handle Diversity Training in the Workplace," *Medium,* June 27, 2018, https://medium.com/s/story/how-white-people-handle-diversity-training-in-the-workplace-e8408d2519f.

28. Brené Brown, "Brené on Shame and Accountability," *Unlocking Us with Brené Brown* Podcast, June 30, 2020, https://podcasts.apple.com/us/podcast/unlocking-us-with-bren%C3%A9-brown/id1494350511?i=1000480887474.

29. "Quotable Quote," Goodreads, accessed October 19, 2020, https://www.goodreads.com/quotes/7273813-do-the-best-you-can-until-you-know-better-then.

30. Annalee Flower Horne, "How 'Good Intent' Undermines Diversity and Inclusion," *The Bias*, September 26, 2017, https://thebias.com/2017/09/26/how-good-intent-undermines-diversity-and-inclusion/.

31. Sue Suh, "'Success Is Not a Solo Sport.' How Workplaces Can Better Support Women of Color," *Time,* December 10, 2019, https://time.com/5746784/minda-harts-the-memo/.

32. "Six Steps to Speak Up," Teaching Tolerance, 2005, https://www.tolerance.org/magazine/publications/speak-up/six-steps-to-speak-up.

33. Steve Andersen (@gokubi), "I created an email template to gently tell colleagues they are using problematic phrases," Twitter, January 15, 2019, 10:03 a.m., https://twitter.com/gokubi/status/1085235929193693184.

34. "Six Steps to Speak Up," Teaching Tolerance.

35. Farhad Manjoo, "Ellen Pao Disrupts How Silicon Valley Does Business," *New York Times*, March 27, 2015, https://www.nytimes.com/2015/03/28/technology/ellen-pao-disrupts-how-silicon-valley-does-business.html.

Chapter 4: Your Network

36. Allison Scott, Freada Kapor Klein, Frieda McAlear, Alexis Martin, and Sonia Koshy, *The Leaky Tech Pipeline: A Comprehensive Framework for Understanding and Addressing the Lack of Diversity across the Tech Ecosystem* (Oakland, CA: Kapor Center for Social Impact, February 2018), http://www.leakytechpipeline.com/wp-content/themes/kapor/pdf/KC18001_report_v6.pdf.

37. Rachel Thomas, Marianne Cooper, Ellen Konar, Megan Rooney, Ashley Finch, Lareina Yee, Alexis Krivkovich, Irina Starikova, Kelsey Robinson, and Rachel Valentino, *Women in the Workplace 2017* (New York and Palo Alto, CA: McKinsey & Company and LeanIn.Org, 2017), https://womenintheworkplace.com/2017.

38. Devon Magliozzi, "Building Effective Networks: Nurturing Strategic Relationships, Especially for Women," The Clayman Institute for Gender Research, April 26, 2016, https://gender.stanford.edu/news-publications/gender-news/building-effective-networks-nurturing-strategic-relationships.

39. Drake Baer, "Why You Need a Diverse Network," August 13, 2013, *Fast Company*, https://www.fastcompany.com/3015552/why-you-need-a-diverse-network.

40. Ivan Misner, "The Importance of Diversity in Networking," *Entrepreneur*, January 26, 2004, https://www.entrepreneur.com/article/68840.

41. Paul Gompers and Silpa Kovvali, "The Other Diversity Dividend," *Harvard Business Review*, July 2018, https://hbr.org/2018/07/the-other-diversity-dividend.

42. "Men, Commit to Mentor Women," Lean In, accessed October 20, 2020, https://leanin.org/mentor-her.

43. "Men, Commit to Mentor Women," Lean In.

44. Nikki Graf, "Sexual Harassment at Work in the Era of #MeToo," Pew Research Center, April 4, 2018, http://www.pewsocialtrends.org/2018/04/04/sexual-harassment-at-work-in-the-era-of-metoo/.

45. Harris O'Malley, "Treating Men like Idiots Is the Wrong Way to Stop Sexual Harassment," *Washington Post*, February 1, 2018, https://www.washingtonpost.com/news/post-nation/wp/2018/02/01/for-men-in-the-metoo-era-the-mike-pence-rule-is-the-easy-way-out/.

46. "Working Relationships in the #MeToo Era," Lean In, accessed October 20, 2020, https://leanin.org/sexual-harassment-backlash-survey-results.

47. Caroline Kitchener, "When It's Hard for Women to Find Male Mentors," *The Atlantic*, August 22, 2017, https://www.theatlantic.com/business/archive/2017/08/women-men-mentorship/537201/.

48. David G. Smith and W. Brad Johnson, *Good Guys: How Men Can Be Better Allies for Women in the Workplace* (Boston, MA: Harvard Business Review Press, 2020).

49. Rachana Bhide, personal communication, September 14, 2020.

50. Rachel Thomas, Marianne Cooper, Ellen Konar, Megan Rooney, Mary Noble-Tolla, Ali Bohrer, Lareina Yee, et al., *Women in the Workplace 2018* (New York and Palo Alto, CA: McKinsey & Company and LeanIn.Org, 2018), accessed November 1, 2018, https://womenintheworkplace.com.

Chapter 5: Organizing and Attending Events

51. Susan Davis, "Before He Was President, Mistaken for a Waiter: a 2003 Obama Meeting," *Wall Street Journal*, November 7, 2008, https://blogs.wsj.com/washwire/2008/11/07/before-he-was-president-mistaken-for-a-waiter-a-2003-obama-meeting/.

52. Derald Wing Sue, "Microaggressions: More Than Just Race," *Psychology Today*, November 17, 2010, https://www.psychologytoday.com/us/blog/microaggressions-in-everyday-life/201011/microaggressions-more-just-race.

53. Rachel Premack, "9 Things People Think Are Fine to Say at Work—but Are Actually Racist, Sexist, or Offensive," *Business Insider*, July 3, 2018, https://www.businessinsider.com/microaggression-unconscious-bias-at-work-2018-6.

54. Dr. Suzanne Wertheim, "The Common Habit That Undermines Organizations' Diversity Efforts," *Fast Company*, May 5, 2016, https://www.fastcompany.com/3060336/the-common-habit-that-undermines-organizations-diversity-efforts.

55. Christine Hauser, "How Professionals of Color Say They Counter Bias at Work," *New York Times*, Dec 12, 2018, https://www.nytimes.com/2018/12/12/us/racial-bias-work.html.

56. Wertheim, "The Common Habit That Undermines Organizations' Diversity Efforts."

57. Theodore Henderson, "How Good Leadership Can Minimize Microaggressions," *Forbes*, March 7, 2017, https://www.forbes.com/sites/forbescoachescouncil/2017/03/07/how-good-leadership-can-minimize-microaggressions/#6b8e19594d70.

58. ADA National Network, *A Planning Guide for Making Temporary Events Accessible to People with Disabilities*, 2015, https://adata.org/publication/temporary-events-guide.

59. Kara Sowles, "Alcohol and Inclusivity," https://docs.google.com/presentation/d/e/2PACX-1vSyiiMJH68OF3BT1w6vqwawHyKEGNF5TTbR1cUf7FWXYadRmZpi9wvv0k-O7glfbhVX0rC7kGIzgKzk/pub?slide=id.p.

60. Justin Murphy, "Risque Photos Cause Controversy at Turtle and Fish Conference," *Democrat and Chronicle*, July 13, 2018, https://www.democratandchronicle.com/story/news/2018/07/13/metoo-jmih-dick-vogt-rochester-herpetologist/782002002/.

61. "Our Commitment to Our Community," Mapbox, accessed November 1, 2018, https://www.mapbox.com/events/code-of-conduct/. Creative Commons Attribution-ShareAlike 4.0 International (CC BY-SA 4.0) license. Reformatted in publishing.

62. Valerie Aurora, *Code of Conduct Training* (San Francisco: Frame Shift Consulting, n.d.), accessed November 1, 2018, https://files.frameshiftconsulting.com/codeofconducttraining.pdf.

Chapter 6: Meetings in the Workplace

63. Claire Zillman, "Ruth Bader Ginsburg Used This Simple Trick to Cut Down on 'Manterrupting'," *Fortune*, April 6, 2017, http://fortune.com/2017/04/06/ruth-bader-ginsburg-supreme-court-advice-interrupting/.

64. Adam Feldman and Rebecca D Gill, "Power Dynamics in Supreme Court Oral Arguments: The Relationship Between Gender And Justice-to-Justice Interruptions," *Taylor Francis Online*, July 31, 2019, https://www.tandfonline.com/doi/abs/10.1080/0098261X.2019.1637309?journalCode=ujsj20.

65. Brandon Tensley, "Mr. Vice President, she's speaking: How Kamala Harris beat the stereotypes during her historic VP debate," CNN, October 8, 2020, https://www.cnn.com/2020/10/08/politics/kamala-harris-pence-debate/index.html.

66. Deborah Tannen, "The Truth about How Much Women Talk—and Whether Men Listen," *Time*, June 28, 2017, http://time.com/4837536/do-women-really-talk-more/.

67. Alexa Renee, "Crowd Erupts at World Science Festival after Moderator Is Called Out for 'Mansplaining,'" *ABC 10*, June 10, 2017, https://www.abc10.com/article/news/uc-davis-professor-had-her-theories-mansplained-during-science-panel/103-446300388.

68. Olivia Leeming (@olivialeeming), "Senior minister Anne Ruston asked if culture for women in parliament has improved...," Twitter, November 9, 2020, 5:25 p.m., https://twitter.com/olivialeeming/status/1325972867771559936.

69. Better Allies, "Tips From the #GHC19 Male Allies Panel, and Other Actions for Allies," *Medium,* October 11, 2019, https://medium.com/@betterallies/tips-from-the-ghc19-male-allies-panel-db659e171ddd.

70. "Meeting Skills," Frame Shift Consulting, accessed September 1, 2018, https://frameshiftconsulting.com/meeting-skills/.

71. Claire Landsbaum, "Obama's Female Staffers Came Up with a Genius Strategy to Make Sure Their Voices Were Heard," *The Cut*, September 13, 2016, https://www.thecut.com/2016/09/heres-how-obamas-female-staffers-made-their-voices-heard.html.

72. Molly Peeples (@astronomolly), "Meeting scene this morning," Twitter, July 18, 2018, 11:24 a.m., https://twitter.com/astronomolly/status/1019618860616568833.

73. Helaine Olen, "Alexandria Ocasio-Cortez Is Not Your Manic Pixie Dream Girl," *Washington Post*, August 10, 2018, https://www.washingtonpost.com/blogs/post-partisan/wp/2018/08/10/alexandria-ocasio-cortez-is-not-your-manic-pixie-dream-girl/.

74. Alexandria Ocasio-Cortez (@AOC), "Just like catcalling, I don't owe a response to unsolicited requests from men with bad intentions," Twitter, August 9, 2018, 6:32 p.m., https://twitter.com/AOC/status/1027729430137827328.

75. Hilary Jerome Scarsella, "Story time. I'm at the airport, working on my laptop, sitting near a guy I just met at a conference this weekend," Facebook, September 22, 2018, https://www.facebook.com/hilary.scarsella/posts/10111805198524389.

76. Elephant in the Valley, accessed June 1, 2018, https://www.elephantinthevalley.com/.

77. Elizabeth Giorgi, personal communication, October 14, 2018.

78. Laura Morgan Roberts and Courtney L. McCluney, "Working from Home While Black," *Harvard Business Review,* June 17, 2020, https://hbr.org/2020/06/working-from-home-while-black.

Chapter 7: Office Housework

79. Elephant in the Valley.

80. Elephant on Madison Avenue, accessed December 1, 2020, https://www.elephantonmadisonavenue.com/sites/default/files/misc-files/EOMA-White-Paper.pdf.

81. Linda Babcock, Maria P. Recalde, and Lise Vesterlund, "Why Women Volunteer for Tasks That Don't Lead to Promotions," *Harvard Business Review*, July 16, 2018, https://hbr.org/2018/07/why-women-volunteer-for-tasks-that-dont-lead-to-promotions.

82. Ruchika Tulshyan, "Women of Color Get Asked to Do More 'Office Housework.' Here's How They Can Say No," *Harvard Business Review*, April 6, 2018, https://hbr.org/2018/04/women-of-color-get-asked-to-do-more-office-housework-heres-how-they-can-say-no.

83. Tulshyan, "Women of Color Get Asked to Do More 'Office Housework.'"

84. Joan C. Williams, "Sticking Women with the Office Housework," *Washington Post*, April 16, 2014, https://www.washingtonpost.com/news/on-leadership/wp/2014/04/16/sticking-women-with-the-office-housework/.

85. Tulshyan, "Women of Color Get Asked to Do More 'Office Housework.'"

Chapter 8: Everyday Language

86. Deb Liu, "The Right Words for the Job: How Gendered Language Affects the Workplace," *Medium*, February 25, 2017, https://medium.com/women-in-product/genderwords-b0be0cc8251f.

87. Anne Janzer, "An Interview with Karen Catlin on Language and Inclusion," Anne Janzer Blog, March 6, 2019, https://annejanzer.com/words-close-doors/.

88. Kim Z. Dale, "40 Gender-Neutral Alternatives to Saying 'You Guys,'" ChicagoNow, May 24, 2017, http://www.chicagonow.com/listing-beyond-forty/2017/05/40-gender-neutral-alternatives-to-saying-you-guys/.

89. Danny Boyle, "London Tube scraps 'ladies and gentlemen' to make announcements gender-neutral," *The Telegraph*, July 13, 2017, https://www.telegraph.co.uk/news/2017/07/13/london-tube-scraps-ladies-gentlemen-make-announcements-gender/.

90. Clár McWeeney, "Let's Talk about the Word 'Lady,'" *Clue*, September 6, 2017, https://helloclue.com/articles/culture/lets-talk-about-word-lady.

91. Neil Schoenherr-Wustl, "Should Targeted Groups Reclaim Slurs To Neutralize Them?," *Futurity*, November 18, 2019, https://www.futurity.org/reappropriation-language-the-slants-2214762-2/.

92. Jeannie Gainsburg, *The Savvy Ally: A Guide for Becoming a Skilled LGBTQ+ Advocate* (Maryland: Rowman & Littlefield, 2020).

93. *Merriam-Webster*, s.v. "they (*pro.*)," accessed November 1, 2018, https://www.merriam-webster.com/dictionary/they.

94. Sinclair Sexsmith (@MrSexsmith), "Dear cis people who put your pronouns on your "hello my name is" nametags: Thank you." Twitter, March 31, 2019, 3:05 p.m., https://twitter.com/MrSexsmith/status/1112475960383684608.

95. Ruchika Tulshyan, "If You Don't Know How to Say Someone's Name, Just Ask," *Harvard Business Review*, January 9, 2020, https://hbr.org/2020/01/if-you-dont-know-how-to-say-someones-name-just-ask.

96. Tulshyan, "If You Don't Know How to Say Someone's Name, Just Ask."

97. Gail Cornwall, "Teachers' Strategies for Pronouncing and Remembering Students' Names Correctly," *KQED,* September 20, 2018, https://www.kqed.org/mindshift/52183/teachers-strategies-for-pronouncing-and-remembering-students-names-correctly.

98. Gainsburg, *The Savvy Ally.*

99. Hannah Denham, "Inclusivity comes to credit cards: Mastercard creates 'True Name' for transgender, non-binary customers," *Washington Post,* June 18, 2019, https://www.washingtonpost.com/business/2019/06/18/mastercard-launching-true-name-its-transgender-nonbinary-cardholders.

100. Rachel Hatzipanagos, "It 'makes you feel invisible'," *Washington Post,* May 2, 2019, https://www.washingtonpost.com/nation/2019/05/02/co-workers-keep-mixing-up-people-color-office-its-more-than-mistake.

101. Jessi Elana Aaron, "'Lame,' 'Stand Up' and Other Words We Use to Insult the Disabled without Even Knowing It," *Washington Post*, May 13, 2015, https://www.washingtonpost.com/posteverything/wp/2015/05/13/lame-stand-up-and-other-words-we-use-to-insult-the-disabled-without-even-knowing-it.

102. Rachel Cohen-Rottenberg, "Doing Social Justice: Thoughts on Ableist Language and Why It Matters," *Disability and Representation*, September 14, 2013, www.disabilityandrepresentation.com/2013/09/14/ableist-language.

103. Lydia X. Z. Brown, "Ableism/Language," Autistic Hoya, last updated December 7, 2016), www.autistichoya.com/p/ableist-words-and-terms-to-avoid.html.

104. Paul Gowder, "What Is a Native American Pow Wow," PowWows.com, July 24, 2011, https://www.powwows.com/what-is-a-pow-wow.

105. Michelle Glauser (@MichelleGlauser), "To avoid being disrespectful by using the word 'powwow,' you can use words such as 'meeting,' 'check-in,' 'stand-up,' 'talk,' 'huddle,' 'one-on-one.'" Twitter, August 30, 2018, 1:52 p.m., https://twitter.com/MichelleGlauser/status/1035238798945181697.

106. "Use These Culturally Offensive Phrases, Questions at Your Own Risk," Indigenous Corporate Training Inc., September 22, 2015, https://www.ictinc.ca/blog/culturally-offensive-phrases-you-should-use-at.

107. Associated Press, "Famed Northern California ski resort changing name, citing offensive word," *Mercury News*, August 25, 2020, https://www.mercurynews.com/2020/08/25/california-ski-resort-changing-name-citing-offensive-word.

108. Security Nerdette (@secnerdette), "Replacing 'whitelist/blacklist' with 'safelist/blocklist' now on," Twitter, August 17, 2017, 5:42 p.m., https://twitter.com/secnerdette/status/898314208097427457.

109. Bron Lewis, "Language Matters," *Nuna*, May 10, 2018, https://blog.nuna.com/language-matters-7fced5d78f8d.

110. Jensen Moore (@MagicalPR), "Added Dr. to my Twitter name today," Twitter, June 17, 2018, 8:41 a.m., https://twitter.com/MagicalPR/status/1008343920269496322.

111. Joseph Epstein, "Is There a Doctor in the White House? Not if You Need an M.D.," *Wall Street Journal*, December 1, 2020, https://www.wsj.com/articles/is-there-a-doctor-in-the-white-house-not-if-you-need-an-m-d-11607727380.

112. Marisa Franco (@MarisaGFranco), "Tip: Instead of asking unfamiliar faces in your department 'are you a student?' ask 'what is your role, here?'" Twitter, August 14, 2018, 11:14 a.m., https://twitter.com/MarisaGFranco/status/1029400971355582464.

113. Dr. Suzanne Wertheim (@WorthwhileRandC), "It's one of the most basic ways to avoid giving an unconscious demotion," Twitter, August 15, 2018, 1:05 p.m., https://twitter.com/WorthwhileRandC/status/1029791229624479744.

114. Security Nerdette (@secnerdette), "I used to think the same way!" Twitter, August 17, 2017, 6:13 p.m., https://twitter.com/secnerdette/status/898321808889266176.

Chapter 9: On Stage

115. AnitaB.org, "Megan Smith - Importance of Diverse Ideas in Gov't GHC15," YouTube video, November 30, 2015, 23:19, https://www.youtube.com/watch?v=ILzUpCA_ozE.

116. Renzo Guinto (@RenzoGuinto), "Just declined an invite to speak in a #COVID19 webinar," Twitter, March 30, 2020, 7:10 a.m., https://twitter.com/RenzoGuinto/status/1244628121090838529.

117. Richard Bradshaw, "My Speaker Rider and Why It's Needed," Friendly Tester, June 12, 2018, https://thefriendlytester.co.uk/2018/06/my-speaker-rider-and-why.

118. Adam Singer (@AdamSinger), "Yo, fellow guys in tech," Twitter, January 29, 2018, 11:23 a.m., https://twitter.com/AdamSinger/status/958027769429950464.

119. Matt May (@mattmay), "If someone hands you a microphone at a conference Q&A," Twitter, October 3, 2018, 1:27 p.m., https://twitter.com/mattmay/status/1047553774884020224.

120. Pluralsight, "Pluralsight LIVE 2017 Mainstage: Joel Spolsky, CEO, Stack Overflow," YouTube video, October 4, 2017, 21:59, www.youtube.com/watch?v=5OJIVp1CgFY.

Chapter 10: Hiring Practices

121. Sohan Murthy, "Measuring Gender Diversity with Data from LinkedIn," *LinkedIn Official Blog*, June 17, 2015, https://blog.linkedin.com/2015/06/17/measuring-gender-diversity-with-data-from-linkedin.

122. Joelle Emerson, "Want to Hire More a More Diverse Set of People? Raise Your Bar." *Medium*, May 11, 2015, https://medium.com/inclusion-insights/want-to-hire-more-diverse-people-raise-your-bar-b5d30f91cbd9.

123. Makinde Adeagbo, "Racial Fault Lines in Silicon Valley," *Medium*, May 25, 2016, https://blog.devcolor.org/racial-fault-lines-in-silicon-valley-390cd0e4a6dc.

124. "Top 10 Ways to Hire the Best for Your Computing Start-Up," National Center for Women in Information Technology, accessed September 29, 2018, https://www.ncwit.org/resources/top-10-ways-hire-best-your-computing-start/top-10-ways-hire-best-your-computing-start.

125. Better Allies (@betterallies), "I use photos of actual employees on my careers page," Twitter, September 5, 2019, 1:08 p.m., https://twitter.com/betterallies/status/1169703873012912128.

126. Entertainment Software Association, "2014 Essential Facts about the Computer and Video Game Industry," 2014, https://www.theesa.com/?s=2014+Essential+Facts+about+the+Computer+and+Video+Game+Industry; Audrey L. Brehm, "Navigating the Feminine in Massively Multiplayer Online Games: Gender in World of Warcraft," *Frontiers in Psychology* 4 (2013): 903, https://doi.org/10.3389/fpsyg.2013.00903.

127. Zapier Jobs page, accessed September 3, 2019, https://zapier.com/jobs.

128. MIT employee resource groups page, accessed September 5, 2019, https://hr.mit.edu/diversity-inclusion/ergs.

129. Change.org post on its LinkedIn page, July 2019, https://www.linkedin.com/posts/change-org_changeorg-is-committed-to-diversity-and-activity-6562451509731225600-ddNt.

130. Claire Ewing-Nelson, "Four Times More Women Than Men Dropped Out of the Labor Force in September," National Women's Law Center, October 2020, https://nwlc-ciw49tixgw5lbab.stackpathdns.com/wp-content/uploads/2020/10/september-jobs-fs1.pdf.

131. Republic Services, "Hiring our Heroes," accessed September 13, 2019, https://republicservices-veterans.jobs.

132. Original study unavailable. See summaries in: Sheryl Sandberg, Lean In: Women, Work, and the Will to Lead, with Nell Scovell (New York: Alfred A. Knopf, 2013); Katty Kay and Claire Shipman, The Confidence Code: The Science and Art of Self-Assurance—What Women Should Know (New York: HarperCollins, 2014).

133. Jo Owen, *How to Lead* (Upper Saddle River, NJ: Prentice Hall, 2011).

134. Tara Sophia Mohr, "Why Women Don't Apply for Jobs Unless They're 100% Qualified," *Harvard Business Review*, August 25, 2014, https://hbr.org/2014/08/why-women-dont-apply-for-jobs-unless-theyre-100-qualified.

135. Webflow job description, accessed October 1, 2020, https://boards.greenhouse.io/webflow.

136. "Who Are the Caregivers?" Family Caregiving Alliance, December 31, 2003, https://www.caregiver.org/women-and-caregiving-facts-and-figures.

137. "Tech Workforce Barriers," Kapor Center for Social Impact, accessed November 1, 2018, http://www.leakytechpipeline.com/barrier/tech-workforce-barriers/.

138. Lauren A. Rivera, "Guess Who Doesn't Fit In at Work," *New York Times*, May 30, 2015, https://www.nytimes.com/2015/05/31/opinion/sunday/guess-who-doesnt-fit-in-at-work.html.

139. Sue Shellenbarger, "The Dangers of Hiring for Cultural Fit," *Wall Street Journal*, September 23, 2019, https://www.wsj.com/articles/the-dangers-of-hiring-for-cultural-fit-11569231000.

140. Textio, "Webinar: How to Fight Diversity Fatigue," Vimeo video, May 14, 2018, 56:24, https://vimeo.com/269693446/624660f941.

141. Lydia Dishman, "How Google, Pinterest, and Others Use Internships to Push Their Diversity Initiatives," *Fast Company*, May 23, 2016, https://www.fastcompany.com/3060118/how-google-pinterest-and-others-use-internships-to-push-their-diversity-i.

142. "Interrupting Bias in Performance Evaluations," Bias Interrupters, accessed November 1, 2018, https://biasinterrupters.org/interrupting-bias-in-performance-evaluations.

143. Abigail Player, Georgina Randsley de Moura, Ana C. Leite, Dominic Abrams, and Fatima Tresh, "Overlooked Leadership Potential: The Preference for Leadership Potential in Job Candidates Who Are Men vs. Women," *Frontiers in Psychology*, April 16, 2019, https://www.frontiersin.org/articles/10.3389/fpsyg.2019.00755/full.

144. GitLab (website), "Interviewing at GitLab," accessed November 18, 2020, https://about.gitlab.com/handbook/hiring/interviewing.

145. Michael Grothaus, "How 'Blind Recruitment' Works And Why You Should Consider It," *Fast Company*, March 14, 2016, https://www.fastcompany.com/3057631/how-blind-recruitment-works-and-why-you-should-consider.

146. Chris Parnin and Matt Shipman, "Tech Sector Job Interviews Assess Anxiety, Not Software Skills," North Carolina State University, July 14, 2020, https://news.ncsu.edu/2020/07/tech-job-interviews-anxiety.

147. Iris Bohnet, "How to Take the Bias out of Interviews," *Harvard Business Review*, April 18, 2016, https://hbr.org/2016/04/how-to-take-the-bias-out-of-interviews.

148. Laszlo Bock, "Here's Google's Secret to Hiring the Best People," *Wired*, April 7, 2015, https://www.wired.com/2015/04/hire-like-google.

149. Laszlo Bock, *Work Rules! Insights from Inside Google That Will Transform How You Live and Lead* (New York: Twelve Books, 2015).

150. re:Work (website), "Google's unbiasing hiring checklists," accessed August 27, 2019, https://docs.google.com/document/d/1_1qvG7ESd2kJj7QJKsUObwMJShswvzurNmpmbM7LE3Y/export?format=pdf.

151. Project Implicit (website), accessed November 1, 2018, https://implicit.harvard.edu.

152. Jason Wong, "Inclusion Interviewing," *Jason Wong's Blog*, July 2, 2018, https://www.attack-gecko.net/2018/07/02/inclusion-interviewing.

153. Lindsay Gellman and Georgia Wells, "What's Holding Back Women in Tech?," *Wall Street Journal*, March 22, 2016, https://www.wsj.com/articles/whats-holding-back-women-in-tech-1458639004.

154. Larissa Shapiro, personal communication, September 20, 2018.

155. Ainsley Robertson, "How we doubled the representation of women in Engineering at Clio," Clio Labs blog, August 28, 2019, https://labs.clio.com/how-we-doubled-the-representation-of-women-in-engineering-at-clio-2d9a4a1a0282.

156. Franklin Leonard (@franklinleonard), "Don't tell people you hired or promoted someone because of their 'diverse perspective.'" Twitter, November 22, 2019, 6:38 p.m., https://twitter.com/franklinleonard/status/1198068279144669185.

157. Franklin Leonard (@franklinleonard), "Saying you hired someone because of their "diverse perspective" is simply code," Twitter, November 22, 2019, 6:43 p.m., https://twitter.com/franklinleonard/status/1198069650816303104.

Chapter 11: Giving Feedback

158. Shelley Correll and Caroline Simard, "Research: Vague Feedback Is Holding Women Back," *Harvard Business Review*, April 29, 2016, https://hbr.org/2016/04/research-vague-feedback-is-holding-women-back.

159. Kieran Snyder, "The Abrasiveness Trap: High-Achieving Men and Women Are Described Differently in Reviews," *Fortune*, August 26, 2014, http://fortune.com/2014/08/26/performance-review-gender-bias.

160. "The State of Black Women in Corporate America 2020," *Lean In,* accessed October 1, 2020, https://leanin.org/research/state-of-black-women-in-corporate-america/introduction.

161. Correll and Simard, "Research: Vague Feedback Is Holding Women Back."

162. Gillian B. White, "Black Workers Really Do Need to Be Twice as Good," *The Atlantic*, October 7, 2015, https://www.theatlantic.com/business/archive/2015/10/why-black-workers-really-do-need-to-be-twice-as-good/409276.

163. National Public Radio, Robert Wood Johnson Foundation, and Harvard T.H. Chan School of Public Health, *Discrimination in America: Experiences and Views of LGBTQ Americans,* November 2017, https://www.rwjf.org/content/dam/farm/reports/surveys_and_pol ls/2017/rwjf441734, 1.

164. Sandy E. James, Jody L. Herman, Susan Rankin, Mara Keisling, Lisa Mottet, and Ma'ayan Anafi, *The Report of the 2015 U.S. Transgender Survey* (Washington: National Center for Transgender Equality, 2016), https://transequality.org/sites/default/files/docs/usts/USTS-Full-Report-Dec17.pdf, 148.

165. Dayana Yochim, "Pride Month: 12 key numbers highlighting the economic status, challenges that LGBTQ people face," *NBC*, June 22, 2020, https://www.nbcnews.com/know-your-value/feature/pride-month-12-key-numbers-highlighting-economic-status-challenges-lgbtq-ncna1231820.

166. David G. Smith, Judith E. Rosenstein, and Margaret C. Nikolov, "How Performance Evaluations Hurt Gender Equality," *Behavioral Scientist*, June 26, 2018, http://behavioralscientist.org/how-performance-evaluations-hurt-gender-equality.

167. Jean Martin, "A Fairer Way to Make Hiring and Promotion Decisions," *Harvard Business Review*, August 13, 2013, https://hbr.org/2013/08/a-fairer-way-to-make-hiring-an.

168. Smith, Rosenstein, and Nikolov, "How Performance Evaluations Hurt Gender Equality."

169. Anna Gifty (@itsafronomics), "So.. today, a professor questioned whether I could pursue a PhD in economics," Twitter, September 5, 2018, 7:27 p.m., https://twitter.com/itsafronomics/status/1037497390859776000.

170. Patty Lopez (@pittrpatt), "When I see someone who I don't know at an event, I assume they belong and introduce myself," Twitter, September 7, 2018, 3:09 p.m., https://twitter.com/pittrpatt/status/1038157229705310209.

171. Mikki Hebl, Christine L. Nittrouer, Abigail R. Corrington, and Juan M. Madera, "How We Describe Male and Female Job Applicants Differently," *Harvard Business Review*, September 27, 2018, https://hbr.org/2018/09/how-we-describe-male-and-female-job-applicants-differently.

172. TEDx Talks, "Are You Biased? I Am | Kristen Pressner | TEDxBasel," YouTube video, August 20, 2016, 8:48, https://www.youtube.com/watch?v=Bq_xYSOZrgU.

173. "The Leaky Tech Pipeline," Kapor Center for Social Impact, accessed November 1, 2018, http://www.leakytechpipeline.com.

174. Elise Gould, *The State of American Wages 2017* (Washington: Economic Policy Institute, March 2018), https://www.epi.org/publication/the-state-of-american-wages-2017-wages-have-finally-recovered-from-the-blow-of-the-great-recession-but-are-still-growing-too-slowly-and-unequally.

175. P.R. Lockhart, "Tuesday is Black Women's Equal Pay Day. Here's what you should know about the gap," Vox, Aug 7, 2018, https://www.vox.com/identities/2018/8/7/17657416/black-womens-equal-pay-day-gender-racial-pay-gap.

176. Stephen Miller, "Black Workers Still Earn Less than Their White Counterparts," June 11, 2020, *SHRM*, https://www.shrm.org/resourcesandtools/hr-topics/compensation/pages/racial-wage-gaps-persistence-poses-challenge.aspx.

177. "The Leaky Tech Pipeline," Kapor Center for Social Impact.

178. Derek Miller, "Occupations with the Largest and Smallest Pay Gap – 2018 Edition," Smart Asset, September 20, 2018, https://smartasset.com/retirement/largest-and-smallest-pay-gap-occupations-2018-edition.

179. Miller, "Occupations with the Largest and Smallest Pay Gap – 2018 Edition."

180. Marcel Schwantes, "The CEO of Salesforce Found Out His Female Employees Were Paid Less Than Men. His Response Is a Priceless Leadership Lesson," *Inc.*, July 26, 2018, https://www.inc.com/marcel-schwantes/the-ceo-of-salesforce-found-out-female-employees-are-paid-less-than-men-his-response-is-a-priceless-leadership-lesson.html.

181. Ivana Kottasová, "The Uk Has a Major Gender Pay Gap Problem. New Data Proves It," *CNN Business*, April 4, 2018, https://money.cnn.com/2018/04/03/news/economy/gender-pay-gap-deadline-uk/index.html.

182. Mani Rolla, "As Women in Tech Gain Experience, Their Pay Gap with Men Gets Worse," *Recode*, April 4, 2018, https://www.recode.net/2018/4/4/17188712/women-tech-salary-job-pay-gap-hired.

183. Benjamin Artz, Amanda Goodall, and Andrew J. Oswald, "Research: Women Ask for Raises as Often as Men, but Are Less Likely to Get Them," *Harvard Business Review*, June 25, 2018, https://hbr.org/2018/06/research-women-ask-for-raises-as-often-as-men-but-are-less-likely-to-get-them.

184. Francesca Fontana, "The Reasons Women Don't Get the Feedback They Need," *Wall Street Journal*, October 12, 2019, https://www.wsj.com/articles/the-reasons-women-dont-get-the-feedback-they-need-11570872601.

185. Lareina Yee, Alexis Krivkovich, Eric Kutcher, Blair Epstein, Rachel Thomas, Ashley Finch, Marianne Cooper, and Ellen Konar, *Women in the Workplace 2016* (Palo Alto, CA, and New York: LeanIn.Org and McKinsey & Company, 2017), https://womenintheworkplace.com/2016.

186. Kim Scott, *Radical Candor: Be a Kick-Ass Boss without Losing Your Humanity* (New York: St. Martin's Press, 2017).

187. Correll and Simard, "Research: Vague Feedback Is Holding Women Back."

188. Juliet Bourke and Andrea Espedido, "Why Inclusive Leaders Are Good for Organizations, and How to Become One," *Harvard Business Review, March 29, 2019,* https://hbr.org/2019/03/why-inclusive-leaders-are-good-for-organizations-and-how-to-become-one.

Chapter 12: Opening Career Doors

189. Stephanie Creary, "How to Be a Better Ally to Your Black Colleagues," *Harvard Business Review,* July 8, 2020, https://hbr.org/2020/07/how-to-be-a-better-ally-to-your-black-colleagues.

190. Oksana Malysheva, "Oksana's Story: Geoffrey Frost," The Corner of the Court Project, June 20, 2018, https://www.cornerofthecourt.com/oksanas-story-geoffrey-frost/.

191. Joan C. Williams and Marina Multhaup, "For Women and Minorities to Get Ahead, Managers Must Assign Work Fairly," *Harvard Business Review*, March 5, 2018, https://hbr.org/2018/03/for-women-and-minorities-to-get-ahead-managers-must-assign-work-fairly.

192. Dulini Fernando, Laurie Cohen, and Joanne Duberley, "What Managers Can Do to Keep Women in Engineering," *Harvard Business Review,* June 12, 2018, https://hbr.org/2018/06/what-managers-can-do-to-keep-women-in-engineering.

193. "Out Of The Comfort Zone," Be Leaderly Blog, January 22, 2019, https://beleaderly.com/stretch-assignments.

194. Kate Rooney and Yasmin Khorram, "Tech companies say they value diversity, but reports show little change in last six years," *CNBC,* June 12, 2020, https://www.cnbc.com/2020/06/12/six-years-into-diversity-reports-big-tech-has-made-little-progress.html.

195. Lori Nishiura Mackenzie and Caroline Simard, "Micro-sponsorship: A tool to combat micro-inequities," Stanford University, March 9, 2016, https://gender.stanford.edu/news-publications/gender-news/micro-sponsorship-tool-combat-micro-inequities.

196. Melissa Locker, "Women of Color Are Less Likely to Get Patents for Their Work," *Fast Company*, July 24, 2018, https://www.fastcompany.com/90207134/women-of-color-are-less-likely-to-get-patents-for-their-work.

197. Catherine Ashcraft, "How Can Companies Promote Innovation with Diverse Employees?," National Center for Women and Information Technology, accessed March 1, 2014, https://www.ncwit.org/resources/how-can-companies-promote-innovation-diverse-employees/how-can-companies-promote.

198. Colleen Flaherty, "Help That Hurts Women," Inside Higher Ed, June 19, 2018, https://www.insidehighered.com/news/2018/06/19/study-finds-recommendation-letters-inadvertently-signal-doubt-about-female; Hebl et al., "How We Describe Male and Female Job Applicants Differently," September 27, 2018, *Harvard Business Review,* https://hbr.org/2018/09/how-we-describe-male-and-female-job-applicants-differently.

199. Tom Hartley (@tom_hartley), "Reading some of my draft references," Twitter, October 8, 2018, 6:22 a.m., https://twitter.com/tom_hartley/status/1049288840047984641.

200. Courtney Connley, "Ambition is not the problem: Women want the top jobs—they just don't get them," *CNBC*, March 5, 2020, https://www.cnbc.com/2020/03/05/why-women-are-locked-out-of-top-jobs-despite-having-high-ambition.html.

201. Barnett and Rivers, "How the 'New Discrimination' Is Holding Women Back."

202. "Interrupting Bias in Performance Evaluations," Bias Interrupters, accessed November 1, 2018, https://biasinterrupters.org/interrupting-bias-in-performance-evaluations/.

203. Rachel Thomas, Marianne Cooper, Ellen Konar, Megan Rooney, Ashley Finch, Lareina Yee, Alexis Krivkovich, Irina Starikova, Kelsey Robinson, and Rachel Valentino, *Women in the Workplace 2017* (New York and Palo Alto, CA: McKinsey & Company and LeanIn.Org, 2017), https://womenintheworkplace.com/2017.

204. Tomas Chamorro-Premuzic, Seymour Adler, and Robert B. Kaiser, "What Science Says about Identifying High-Potential Employees," *Harvard Business Review*, October 3, 2017, https://hbr.org/2017/10/what-science-says-about-identifying-high-potential-employees.

205. Laszlo Bock, *Work Rules!*.

206. Cecilia Kang, "Google Data-Mines Its Approach to Promoting Women," *Washington Post*, April 2, 2014, https://www.washingtonpost.com/news/the-switch/wp/2014/04/02/google-data-mines-its-women-problem.

207. Freada Kapor Klein, "What's It Like to Be a Female Tech Entrepreneur?," *Medium*, September 14, 2018, https://medium.com/kapor-the-bridge/whats-it-like-to-be-a-female-tech-entrepreneur-a170a99089eb.

208. Sharethrough, "The Inclusive Leader - Developing Diverse Teams // Jill Wetzler // Calibrate 2017," YouTube video, November 10, 2017, 38:21, https://www.youtube.com/watch?v=PDepSAbhNuc.

Chapter 13: A Call to Action

209. Matt Rosoff, "A Google Employee Posted a 10-Page Treatise about Bias, and People Are Outraged," *CNBC*, August 5, 2017, https://www.cnbc.com/2017/08/05/google-engineer-posts-anti-diversity-treatise.html.

210. Sophia Chen, "Physicists Condemn Sexism through 'Particles for Justice,'" *Wired*, October 5, 2018, https://www.wired.com/story/physicists-condemn-sexism-through-particles-for-justice.

211. Raven Baxter, as told to Jackie Flynn Mogensen, "I'm a Black Female Scientist. On My First Day of Work, a Colleague Threatened to Call the Cops on Me.," *Mother Jones,* June 15, 2020, https://www.motherjones.com/anti-racism-police-protest/2020/06/blackintheivory-racism-academia-science-stem.

212. Katherine Long, "Why Don't Women Code? A UW Lecturer's Answer Draws Heat," *Seattle Times*, June 22, 2018, https://www.seattletimes.com/seattle-news/education/why-dont-women-code-a-uw-lecturers-answer-draws-heat.

213. Shelly Banjo and Dina Bass, "On Diversity, Silicon Valley Failed to Think Different," *Bloomberg Businessweek*, August 3, 2020, https://www.bloomberg.com/news/articles/2020-08-03/silicon-valley-didn-t-inherit-discrimination-but-replicated-it-anyway.

214. Audrey Murrell, "On the Tennis Court and in the Workplace: When Unconscious Bias Isn't Unconscious," *Forbes*, September 20, 2018, https://www.forbes.com/sites/audreymurrell/2018/09/20/on-the-tennis-court-and-in-the-workplace-when-unconscious-bias-isnt-unconscious.

215. Michelle Kim, "How to Manage Your Team in Times of Political Trauma," *Medium,* September 4, 2017, https://medium.com/awaken-blog/managing-teams-in-times-of-political-trauma-what-to-do-what-to-say-to-boost-psychological-safety-b5782969d6fa.

216. Corey Ponder, "I'm tired of the loop, america.," Corey Ponder's Blog, June 4, 2020, https://www.coreyponder.com/post/tired-of-the-loop.

217. Tom Peters (@tom_peters), "Bosses: Who are the four folks whose development path you will have dramatically effected by 12/31/18?," Twitter, December 29, 2017, 11:43 a.m., https://twitter.com/tom_peters/status/946783783835066368.

218. Smith and Johnson, *Good Guys*.

219. Better Allies (@betterallies), "During #BlackHistoryMonth, my goal as a white person is to take actions that will last year-round," Twitter, February 6, 2019, 6:55 a.m., https://twitter.com/betterallies/status/1093161283644313601.

220. Katrina Jones (@Katrina_HRM), "Suggestion here - since these actions are in recognition of Black History Month," Twitter, February 6, 2019, 7:15 a.m., https://twitter.com/Katrina_HRM/status/1093166242054135810.

Bonus Chapter

221. Kristen Pressner, personal communication, April 23, 2018.

222. David Smith, personal communication, April 23, 2018.

223. Jennifer Brown, personal communication, April 24, 2018.

224. Cath Jones, personal communication, April 24, 2018.

Epilogue

225. Concerned Feminists (@concernedfems), "So this is happening. #ghc14 #ghcmanwatch," Twitter, October 8, 2014, 8:31 p.m., https://twitter.com/concernedfems/status/520023816769388547.

226. Cate Huston and Karen Catlin, "Tech's Male 'Feminists' Aren't Helping," *Daily Beast*, December 8, 2014, https://www.thedailybeast.com/techs-male-feminists-arent-helping.

227. Leigh Honeywell, "Bingo and Beyond," hypatia dot ca, September 23, 2015, https://hypatia.ca/2015/09/23/bingo-and-beyond/.

228. The 3% Movement, "Manbassador Bingo," 2015, https://www.3percentmovement.com/resources/manbassador-bingo.

Made in United States
Orlando, FL
31 August 2022